Praise for *Poetry in Place*

In a time of dire ecological distress it is heartening to encounter an anthology with such a rich diversity of voices—Indigenous, immigrant, settler—all engaging with place, and in ways that depart from its usual function as merely the backdrop or setting for human endeavour. With their wide range of subjects and styles these poems testify to the possibility of living outside the vicious 'regime of property' (as Emmanuel Levinas calls it) that reduces all our relations to versions of possession. Rebecca Solnit and others have emphasized that hope is a practice and not a calculus of the odds. By giving voice to these ardent acts of attention, *Poetry in Place* helps us sustain that difficult practice of hope.

—**Don McKay**, twice winner of the Governor General's Literary Award for Poetry, and winner of the 2024 Griffin Poetry Prize's Lifetime Recognition Award

Twenty-first-century people generally have a tenuous relation to place. Even for those whose ancestors lived here for generations, this land between Lakes Huron, Ontario, and Erie moves and changes, in our minds, in our laws, and under our feet. The poets in this volume—Indigenous, immigrant, settler—help us ground ourselves in this living, changing land by paying written attention to its cycles, beings, and intelligence. We need their words to learn where we are, who our neighbours are, what happened here, let alone what's happening now, how to cooperate, and how to return the gifts we've been given.

—**Daniel Coleman**, Professor of English and Cultural Studies, McMaster University; author, *Yardwork: A Biography of an Urban Place*

In engendering love and curiosity through poetry, and uncovering a deeper understanding and passion for land, water and culture, readers will surely respond to *Poetry in Place* by searching out more and rising to take action on ecological and cultural restoration—a grand achievement.

—**Brian McHattie**, former Hamilton City Councillor, Parks Canada and Environment and Climate Change staffer, and mostly retired professional planner

Poets read the landscape like a book, and conjure from it words that 'light up the terrain,' as Margaret Avison might have put it. The deep looking and soundings in *Poetry in Place* inspire to make us all attentive in this manner and derive from its word-making a hope that is latent in *this* place at *this* time.

—**Sally Ito**, Japanese-Canadian poet and translator; most recent book of poetry, *Heart's Hydrography*

POETRY IN PLACE

Poetry and Environmental Hope in a Southern Ontario Bioregion

ESSENTIAL ANTHOLOGIES SERIES 18

Canada Council for the Arts
Conseil des Arts du Canada

ONTARIO ARTS COUNCIL
CONSEIL DES ARTS DE L'ONTARIO
an Ontario government agency
un organisme du gouvernement de l'Ont

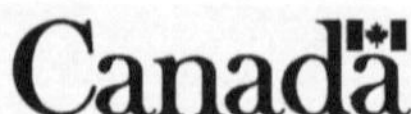

Guernica Editions Inc. acknowledges the support of the Canada Council for the Arts and the Ontario Arts Council. The Ontario Arts Council is an agency of the Government of Ontario.

We acknowledge the financial support of the Government of Canada.

POETRY IN PLACE

Poetry and Environmental Hope in a Southern Ontario Bioregion

Deborah Bowen, editor
Noah Van Brenk, assistant editor

GUERNICA EDITIONS

TORONTO—CHICAGO—BUFFALO—LANCASTER (U.K.)

2025

Guernica Founder, Antonio D'Alfonso

Michael Mirolla, editor
Cover and interior design: Errol F. Richardson
Front Cover Image: Lynn Bergsma Friesen

Guernica Editions Inc.
1241 Marble Rock Rd., Gananoque (ON), Canada K7G 2V4
2250 Military Road, Tonawanda, N.Y. 14150-6000 U.S.A.
www.guernicaeditions.com

Distributors:
Independent Publishers Group (IPG)
600 North Pulaski Road, Chicago IL 60624
University of Toronto Press Distribution (UTP)
5201 Dufferin Street, Toronto (ON), Canada M3H 5T8

First edition.
Printed in Canada.

Legal Deposit – First Quarter
Library of Congress Catalog Card Number: 2024945650
Library and Archives Canada Cataloguing in Publication
Title: Poetry in place : poetry and environmental hope in a southern Ontario bioregion / Deborah Bowen, editor ; Noah Van Brenk, assistant editor.
Other titles: Poetry in place (Guernica)
Names: Bowen, Deborah C., editor.
Series: Essential anthologies series ; 18.
Description: Series statement: Essential anthologies series ; 18
Identifiers: Canadiana 2024045278X | ISBN 9781771839716 (softcover)
Subjects: LCSH: Nature—Poetry. | LCSH: Grand River (Ont.)—Poetry. | LCSH: Ontario, Lake (N.Y. and Ont.)—Poetry. | LCSH: Ontario, Southwestern—Poetry. | CSH: Canadian poetry (English)—21st century. | LCGFT: Nature poetry. | LCGFT: Poetry.
Classification: LCC PS8287.N38 P64 2025 | DDC C811/.608036097132—dc23

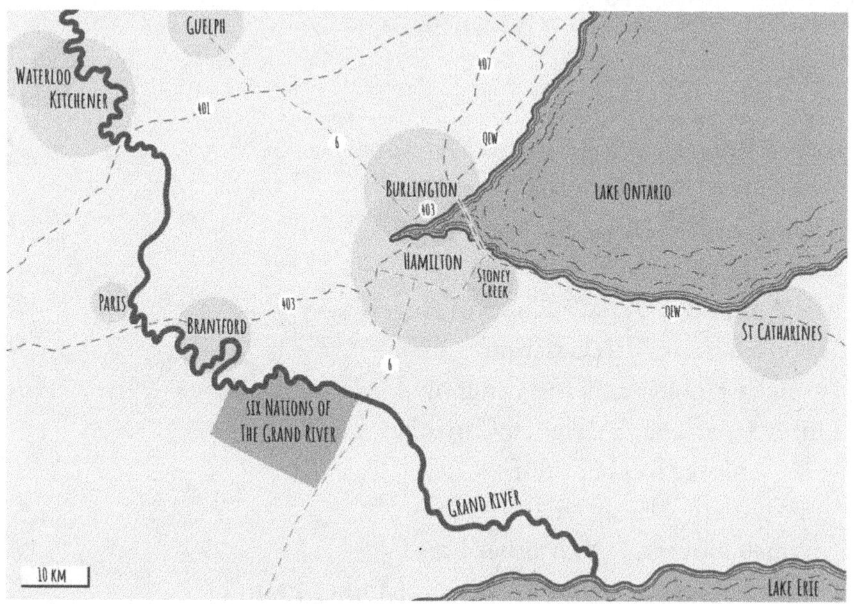

The poetry in this book comes from the area covered by this map,
between the Grand River and the westernmost tip of Lake Ontario.
Recognizing the Between the Lakes Treaty No. 3 of 1792,
which covers much wider territory,
we have described this smaller area as
'The Land Between the Waters.'

Contents

Food

Future Perfect Tense

** starred poems are also available in visual or oral format via the QR code below under **Additional Resource: Playlist.***

Poets in Place: interviews

Coda:
Three Hamiltonian city poems

And a last word

Additional resource

Playlist of visual and oral presentations

Introducing *Poetry in Place*

This is a book of poems by and interviews with immigrants, settlers, and Indigenous writers who live in a very specific territory: what we have described as the "Land Between the Waters" of Lake Ontario and the Grand River, west of Toronto and east of London, in southern Ontario—a region of great ecological and cultural diversity. This area of Ontario has some of the most rich and fertile soil in the whole of Canada; it also has a superabundance of histories and stories. As the Indigenous writer and scholar Lee Maracle has put it, "Imagine, 168 nations of peoples are in Toronto, probably 100 nations in the Guelph area. All kinds of knowledge, all kinds of stories, all kinds of art, all kinds of sensibility, religions, philosophies: we could learn from that. We could put these things together. We could recreate the world."[1]

In this anthology you will find poems based in this particular landscape by more than forty different poets—poets of many different ages, ethnicities, and backgrounds, some new to publishing and some well-established authors—as well as interviews with all of these poets. Any relation to the land will be enmeshed with the stresses of history, politics, and economics, and so any gathering of work about this place will necessarily reflect that complexity, sometimes difficult, sometimes hopeful. In fact many of the poets here have made the decision to have hope for our natural environment and our future—hope that we always need, but especially in these days of climate disruption, environmental degradation and biodiversity loss, of reckoning with the legacy and consequences of colonialism, and, in 2020-22 as we were gathering the majority of the poems, of global pandemic. "We could recreate the world," Maracle says. And in the course of that turn to recreation, what might it be that the natural world itself has to say to us? How can we hear its voices? It is often pointed out that history is told by the

---

[1] Lee Maracle, University of Waterloo Indigenous Speakers Series, Oct. 3, 2018 https://medium.com/@gracelynn.lau/a-dish-with-one-spoon-treaty-intact-memories-seeking-to-contribute-a3f39dabd6d6 and, with Bill Coleman, https://www.youtube.com/watch?v=NfE34zzu2a8

victor—but what if, instead, it were told by the land and the people and creatures who live there, as they navigate their relation with this place?

In these times

In her interview later in this collection, local Métis poet Arwen Roussell says, "I honour the land with my life because my body is the land … I'm not separate from the land. When I touch my feet to the earth, I feel like I'm touching my own self." Seasoned Canadian environmentalist David Suzuki has affirmed this membership too: "We have to recognize that we are interconnected with each other, with nature, even with the rocks and waters that form our home."[2] In a spirit of radical optimism, Suzuki declared in 2021 that "Those of us who care outnumber the short-sighted, profit-driven and careless, and those who heed them out of fear and ignorance. We must make ourselves heard."[3] The urgency of this call, which had already been magnified by the climate crisis, became even more audible to an even wider audience because of the pandemic; it could be heard right at the heart of Western capitalism. Thus, at the early height of the pandemic in 2020, American ecologist David Abram wrote, "We can take rich advantage of this time to become more deeply of place, more deeply of the local earth," because "our real collective flesh is that of the Earth itself, this immense spherical metabolism in which we're all embedded and embodied."[4] And British environmentalist Michael McCarthy observed that "nature, which has been lost to sight so widely, has suddenly been made visible once again by the pandemic, by the extraordinary circumstance of the anthropause, and most of all, by people's own need to seek out nature as a relief from unprecedented stress."[5]

In his biography of the great environmental activist Wendell Berry, Ragan Sutterfield describes how "It is by humility […] that we join the membership of creation in acceptance that we are a part of the world

---

2 David Suzuki, "U.S. Crisis shows need to speak truth to power." Online blog "Science Matters," January 15, 2021.

3 Suzuki, ibid.

4 David Abram, "The Ecology of Perception," Interview, *Emergence Magazine*, August 2, 2020.

5 Michael McCarthy, "The Coronavirus Pandemic and the Invisibility of Nature," *Emergence Magazine*, Dec. 6, 2020.

rather than an individual struggling against it."[6] If Berry is right, even the recognition of our need of "nature" requires humility. Linzey Corridon says in interview in this collection, "We often talk about equity and equality as existing exclusively between *homo sapiens*, but then we completely refuse to acknowledge how the lands on which we settle should be treated in a similar fashion." There is a virtue to be learned here—a posture to acquire. And in a profound sense it is the posture of the poet.

Poetry as listening

Poets customarily look for what nature writer Robert MacFarlane has called "a language of purchase and attention."[7] For poets are bound to pay attention. Whatever their subject, says Marilyn McEntyre, "Poets slow us down. They teach us to stop and go in before we go on. They play at the edges of mystery, holding a tension between line and sentence, between sense and reason, between the epiphanic and the deeply, comfortingly familiar."[8] This kind of stance toward the world involves a posture of careful listening. Oftentimes we don't hear the natural world speaking because we don't slow down enough to listen, or pay enough attention to learn how it speaks. In this book you will find poets who have listened not only to the land, but also to water, and trees, and birds, and wild creatures, and flowers and plants, and insects, and have learned deeply about how this natural world is essential for human flourishing through farming and gardening and the production of food. As Chief Stacey Laforme has written, "Remember, we need the Earth: she does not need us."[9] The very fact that poetry is distinctive, different in sound, texture, and form from everyday writing and speaking, is significant here: as one poet in our anthology, Adam Dickinson, has put it, "What is the most extreme form of writing that humans have developed? It's poetry.

---

6 Ragan Sutterfield, *Wendell Berry and the Given Life* (Franciscan Media, 2017).

7 Robert MacFarlane, in "Speaking the Anthropocene," interview with Emmanuel Vaughan-Lee, *Emergence Magazine*, Aug. 2020. https://emergencemagazine.org/story/speaking-the-anthropocene/

8 Marilyn McEntyre, *When Poets Pray* (Eerdmans, 2019).

9 Chief R. Stacey Laforme, *Living in the Tall Grass: Poems of Reconciliation* (UpRoute/Durvile, 2017), p. 18.

Poetry lives at the absolute limits of expression, so poetry is a highly appropriate form of response to these questions of environmental ethics."[10] Poetry by its specificity and its profound energy can help us pay attention to the interdependent relationships of the human with the land and its other creatures. In terms of this anthology, we are particularly grateful that we have been able to include the specific poetic vision of four poets who passed away before publication could be completed: Daniel David Moses, David Haskins, Klyde Broox, and Sheryl Loeffler. Our hope is that their voices in this collection, both in poetry and in the prose of their interviews, will live on in the vibrant words they have left to us to convey their particular relationships within the natural world.

Indigenous knowledge, spiritual grounding

The relationship between the health of the whole natural world and the health of the humans who are part of it is key to this growing understanding, or perhaps more accurately this rediscovery, rather late in the Age of the Anthropocene, that ecosystems, including both humans and other creatures, are fundamentally interdependent. This interdependence is something that Indigenous peoples have known and celebrated for thousands of years. And it has a deeply ethical frame, which Western science has ignored to humanity's peril, but is now beginning to recognize and reckon with. As Suzuki wrote in February 2021:

> In many ways, Indigenous knowledge is more encompassing and profound than [Western] science. … It's critical for a people's survival and has been tested by their presence over thousands of years … the element of reciprocity, of responsibility, is missing in contemporary science, and society in general.[11]

---

10 Adam Dickinson, in interview with the editors (at Brock U, St Catharines), August 2017.

11 David Suzuki, "Finding wisdom in science and Indigenous knowledge," in the online blog "Science Matters," February 12, 2021.

It is, then, particularly appropriate, given the title *Poetry in Place*, that this anthology includes poetry by several local Indigenous poets, and that their voices and their perspectives are honoured in the interviews of the last part of the book.[12] In her interview, Chandra Maracle explains that, "In Haudenosaunee cosmology, it's nearly impossible to talk about the Earth without referring to her as our Mother, and that makes a difference in how we treat her." Those of us who have grown up under Western capitalism have so much to learn about the significance of a reciprocal relationship with the earth—what Potawotomi writer and scientist Robin Wall Kimmerer calls a "gift economy," rather than an extractive or commodity economy. Kimmerer writes, "I imagine if we acknowledged that everything we consume is the gift of Mother Earth, we would take better care of what we are given. Mistreating a gift has emotional and ethical gravity as well as ecological resonance," because "the currency in a gift economy is relationship, which is expressed as gratitude, as interdependence and the ongoing cycles of reciprocity."[13]

Many spiritual leaders are now acknowledging this interconnected responsibility as well. Given the nominally Christian background of most settlers in North America over the last 250 years, and despite the ravages of Western capitalist exploitation, it's important to remember that the Judeo-Christian founding documents honour the earth, not least because it has been given to all of God's creatures to enjoy. The present Pope, Francis, has written extensively about the vital necessity of recognizing our deep physical and ethical connections with the earth.[14] And Rowan Williams, the former Archbishop of Canterbury, has written, "Our present ecological crisis [has] a great deal to do with our failure to think of the world as existing in relation to the mystery of God, not just as a huge warehouse of

---

12 What we have in this book designated the "Land Between the Waters" of Lake Ontario and the Grand River lies within the traditional territory of Indigenous nations, as recognized in the 1792 Between the Lakes Treaty No. 3 with the Mississaugas of the Credit First Nation. But much of the land is still contested, for instance in terms of the outstanding land rights agreed to in the Haldimand Treaty of 1784 with the Six Nations Confederacy.

13 Robin Wall Kimmerer, "The Serviceberry: An Economy of Abundance," Emergence Magazine, Dec. 20, 2020.

14 See Pope Francis, *Laudato 'Si: On Care for Our Common Home* (Boston: Pauline Books & Media, 2015), and its addendum in October 2023.

stuff to be used for our convenience."[15] In fact all of the world's great religious traditions have strong ecological beliefs, such that, whether or not a specific religion would describe the natural world as the direct creation of a god, it is incumbent on human beings to act in it with care and responsibility.[16] Some of the poets in this book have specific spiritual commitments, some do not, but all are aware of the mysterious reality of the natural world and its claims to be taken seriously on its own account. Many write of how profoundly they are affected by the natural landscape. Plains Cree poet Corri Daniels, for many years a resident on the Land Between the Waters, puts it this way: "I feel spiritually grounded when I'm standing beside two-hundred-year-old cedar trees. That's medicine." Each poet has the opportunity to speak to these and related issues in the interviews that make up the final section of our book.

This land, this place

Why does the poetry of place matter? Perhaps because, as philosopher-poet Karen Houle says here, "one is always in an exact eco-geographical location: on treaty land, in a watershed." But why this particular place, this Land Between the Waters? This pocket of southern Ontario, about an hour's drive west of Toronto around the western tip of Lake Ontario, is bounded to the east by the lake, to the west by the Grand River and the Niagara Escarpment, and includes the cities of Guelph, Hamilton, Kitchener/Waterloo, Brantford, and St Catharines. As part of the "Golden Horseshoe" from Toronto to Niagara Falls, it lies in the most densely populated and industrialized area in Canada, a region that encompasses major industry, significant farming and fruit-growing, a rich post-secondary educational landscape, and rapidly-increasing housing development, as well as the largest First Nations reserve in the country,[17] with all the freighted history that such a reserve implies.

---

15 Rowan Williams, *Tokens of Trust: An Introduction to Christian Belief* (Canterbury P, 2007).

16 The fact that Western religion was used to establish the Doctrine of Discovery and provided the rationale to seize and exploit Indigenous lands is a shameful inheritance that present-day Christian believers must deplore.

17 The Six Nations of the Grand River comprise over twenty-seven thousand members, of whom almost half live on the reserve itself; the smaller though once dominant nation of the Mississaugas of the Credit (presently around three thousand members, about one-third living on the reserve) occupies adjacent land.

The region has traditionally supplied fertile agricultural land as well as easy access to water routes. It is shot through with the complex and troubled history of Indigenous territory and white settlement, as well as that of other ethnic groups, including the Black communities that arose in the mid-nineteenth century as a result of both the Ontario terminus of the Underground Railway and the arrival of Black along with white loyalists from the United States. A region often maligned as uninteresting, it can instead be viewed as deeply compelling, as a significant site for the industrialization of the Great Lakes, the displacement of Indigenous peoples, and the ongoing influx of immigrant communities from a shifting global population, as well as including what Dickinson describes as "an international border with the last remaining superpower on the planet"—this place, he says, is "a kind of Ground Zero."[18] It happens also to be an area that is rich in creative writers.

Given both its historical and contemporary complexity, we might say that this is a place that needs to be spoken for, that needs to be seen and heard anew. Perhaps that is the manifesto of our collection. For, as literary critic Alan Jacobs has put it, "When one loses connection to a *particular* landscape, one loses the language appropriate to that landscape, and once the language has evaporated, one's vision blurs or one grows altogether blind."[19] The relationship between seeing and hearing is mysterious and powerful. And what, after all, constitutes a language—must it be limited to an anthropocentric concept? As poet John Terpstra considers the landscape of this area, he muses: "I wonder now if the world we see around us, the rock, trees, water, etc., are each forms of speech, different languages, that we must learn to hear and understand if we are to enter and tell the story."

Speaking for the land: the local story in brief

From the start it's important to recognize that the Land Between the Waters—bounded by two Great Lakes as well as by the Grand River—

---

18 Adam Dickinson, in interview with the editors (at Brock U, St Catharines), August 2021.

19 Alan Jacobs, "The Counter-Desecration Phrasebook"—review of Robert MacFarlane's *Landmarks* (Penguin Random House, 2016), in *Books and Culture*, March/April 2016.

is home to some of the richest soil in Canada. And it's worth noting that it takes approximately one hundred years for one inch of that topsoil to form. For thousands of years this land has been home to Indigenous peoples whose agricultural methods were restorative. By contrast, white settlement here from the eighteenth century onwards introduced an invasive way of life, a mentality of conquest over a wild landscape, and a concept of private land ownership that disallowed the hunting and foraging and nomadic farms of the Indigenous nations. The Mississaugas of the Credit, whose traditional territory spans much of modern-day Southwestern Ontario, negotiated eight treaties with the British government between 1781 and 1820. One of these treaties, the 1784 Between the Lakes Treaty No.3 (ratified in 1792), allowed the Crown to grant to the Haudenosaunee "People of the Longhouse," many of whom had arrived in the area after supporting the British in the American Revolution, a parcel of land known as the Haldimand Tract, stretching ten kilometers each side of the Grand River.[20] But over the years all of these lands were encroached on, sold up, and generally not respected. By the time the British authorities officially created a protected reserve for the Haudenosaunee Six Nations in 1847, it was less than a tenth of the size of the original settlement of land granted only sixty years before. And despite the fact that the Mississaugas of the Credit are the Treaty and Territory holders for the lands referred to in this book, their lands were lost to settlers; in a strange twist of fate, they were invited by the Six Nations Confederacy back onto their previous lands—their reserve lies on land adjacent to the reserve of the Six Nations of the Grand River.

Meantime, white land grants were organized into a grid system of townships that reflected the European idea of ownership, and is still evidenced in our road patterns to this day. This attitude to land was reinforced among both European and American settlers by their Enlightenment understanding of Christianity, which saw the human

---

[20] The chief negotiator for the land grant to the Six Nations was Joseph Brant ('Thayendanegea'). For more on this history, see Rick Monture, *We Share Our Matters: Two Centuries of Writing and Resistance at Six Nations of the Grand River* (U of Manitoba P, 2014), pp. 15-17 and 156.

as an independent rational being for whom possession of property was a right. The Niagara Peninsula was one of three principal gateways for many Loyalist immigrants, both Black and white, to enter Ontario, and in the first decades of the nineteenth century there was also a big wave of tens of thousands of immigrants from Britain and Europe. All these settlers seem to have been united in their view of "nature" as needing to be subdued and dominated in the name of "progress." One British visitor in the 1830s commented that settlers viewed trees as enemies that must be eradicated, because they had to be cleared to create open arable land.[21] As a result, trees older than 200 years are very rare in this area. At the same time, in another kind of ecological imperialism, settlers often brought seeds with them and told those who would arrive after them to follow suit. So, whereas the First Nations peoples believed in honouring their origins by maintaining connections with the natural world, European migration to and settler colonialism in our area were both anthropologically and ecologically foreign and invasive.

Nevertheless, by the 1840s the Land Between the Waters had emerged as a prime agricultural belt in Canada; the area north-east of Hamilton was producing the highest amount of wheat per acre in the whole country at that time. Hamilton's lying at the western tip of Lake Ontario made it a valuable trading centre for ship traffic, and in the mid-nineteenth century it also became a centre of railway building, so that it grew to dominate industrial production through its foundries and grist mills and ports, rivalled only by Toronto well into the twentieth century. All along, the industrialization boom of the second half of the nineteenth century demonstrated a continuation of settler-colonial attitudes and agricultural practices. But as the decades passed, farmers were running out of land to farm and labourers were attracted to city wages, so that by 1940 there were more Canadians living in urban centres than in rural ones, and farms were expected to serve the needs of the cities.

---

21 See Peter Baskerville, *Sites of Power: A Concise History of Ontario* (Oxford U P, 2005), p. 65, and John Mohawk's Prologue to *The White Roots of Peace*, by Paul A.W. Wallace (Satanac Lake, N Y: Chauncy P, 1986), p. xix.

And, of course, the industrial development across this whole area had devastating ecological effects, as rivers were buried and forests, grasslands, and wetlands were paved over with impermeable materials. Whereas the region pre-European settlement was 80% covered in deciduous forest, now there is only 15% forest cover, and natural habitats have been splintered into fragments between private property. Water was also affected by urbanization: areas like Hamilton Harbour gradually filled with toxic industrial waste, and the water in the Grand River and the local Great Lakes suffered from fertilizer pollution that caused mass die-offs of fish. Eventually, faced with these devastations, people began to pay attention to the problems that industrialization was causing. The four local conservation authorities were created out of a particular concern for watershed conservation;[22] more recently there has been work on remediating Hamilton Harbour, the largest contaminated site in the Great Lakes, and on managing invasive species. The Royal Botanical Gardens was founded in Burlington in 1941. Guelph has an Arboretum of 400 acres and a city-wide commitment to sustainability and renewable energy. In Waterloo there is a seedbank of 3000 varieties of grain, fruit and flower seeds, and the Waterloo Institute for Sustainable Energy conducts research into less detrimental energy production. Though it is by many considered to be too weak, Ontario does have a provincial Climate Change Strategy, and the Greenbelt Act of 2005 remains in place to curb the expansion of urban growth into agricultural and natural areas. Thus, even though the majority of Ontarians no longer have any substantial direct connection to the landscape they dwell in, and even though the present Ontario government tried (unsuccessfully) to claim back large swaths of the Greenbelt for housing development, many people are waking up to the importance of caring for our soil, water, and forest. And in fact this isn't for the first time: "It's pretty telling that the [early] settlers themselves saw that we were creating

---

22 See The Grand River Conservation Authority (www.grandriver.ca), Hamilton Conservation Authority (www.conservationhamilton.ca), The Bruce Trail Conservancy (https://brucetrail.org/), The Niagara Peninsula Conservation Authority (www.npca.ca), and Conservation Halton (www.conservationhalton.ca).

a monster," poet-historian Elizabeth Tessier observes in interview, referencing the later life of 19th-century English-Canadian author and naturalist Catherine Parr Traill.[23]

Meanwhile the population of the Land Between the Waters has changed radically over the last fifty years, with much greater immigration from non-European countries,[24] and in the future we should expect to see increasing numbers of climate refugees along with the rest.[25] Canada's reputation as a country friendly to immigrants and refugees reinforces the fact that we will need to continue to look for ways to better steward the land and its resources so that it can support all who depend on them. Dickinson articulates in interview the urgency in the Anthropocene of understanding this physical interconnectedness with our natural environment: "Place is no longer just about where you live, but about the way in which a body absorbs its environment, becomes written over by its environment, and passes that environment down through generations. The body is a trans-local place, a kind of mobile bioregion."

A glossary for clear vision

And so we need to exercise our faculties of re-cognition anew about the land under our feet, for both societal and personal health, and for a future that includes not only care for the land but also justice for the Indigenous peoples whose relationships to this land have been so deeply unsettled by colonial settlement. We believe that poetry is a vital part of this re-visioning. As Doug Sikkema says here, "I don't hold the hope that literature or beauty is going to save the world—but I do think it can *address* evil, and maybe part of restoration can happen that way." Perhaps these poems may help readers "feel

---

[23] Tessier describes how "Catherine Parr Traill initially wrote about how to struggle against the wilderness, but near the end of her life she became an environmental activist, questioning what settlers were doing to the world around them, such as cutting down irreplaceable trees."

[24] For instance, there are immigrants in this area from China, Columbia, Ghana, Guatemala, India, Iran, Iraq, Kenya, Korea, Pakistan, Palestine, Syria, and Vietnam, to name just a few of the countries represented.

[25] Many climate projections actually describe Canada as having great potential to continue to take people in, since a number of areas in this country that are currently too cold to support a large population will become warmer arable land with significant water resources. See https://climateatlas.ca/climate-change-maps-agriculture.

understood in some way, but also kind of jostled," Elise Arsenault told us, so that "they feel seen while also seeing the world with a little more awe, nuance, and curiosity."

This clearer kind of seeing is not just a private and personal issue. Haudenosaunee scholar Rick Monture from Six Nations has written that, when they recall their spiritual relationship to the earth, Indigenous peoples see that "relationships found in the natural world [can] become activated in the human world as means of social and political thought."[26] One political commentator has even suggested that true patriotism is "the virtue of those who know where in particular their time on earth is spent [...]. It is a virtue of concreteness."[27] After all, seeing and hearing are both **placed** capacities. Robert Macfarlane argues in *Landmarks* that "We need now, urgently, a Counter-Desecration Phrasebook that would comprehend the world—a glossary of enchantment for the whole earth, which would allow nature to talk back and would help us to listen."[28] As John Terpstra declares in the penultimate poem of our collection, "whatever our blood or background, our belief, / whichever street we live on, / we share this dish ..." Our hope is that the poetry in this volume will go some way towards providing a glossary of enchantment for this area, this Land Between the Waters—and that these poems may also inspire you to look and listen anew in whatever land it is where you yourself are placed.

Deborah Bowen, Hamilton, August 2024

I am very grateful to Liane Miedema Brown and Noah Van Brenk for much of the background research in this introduction into the natural and social history of the Land Between the Waters, to Gary Barwin for helpfully radical suggestions for revision, and to Brian McHattie for his assistance in clarifying many points of Indigenous history.

---

[26] Rick Monture, *We Share Our Matters: Two Centuries of Writing and Resistance at Six Nations of the Grand River* (U of Manitoba P, 2014).

[27] Oliver O'Donovan, "Political Authority and Law," *Breaking Ground* symposium, Jan 8, 2021.

[28] Robert Macfarlane, *Landmarks* (Penguin Random House, 2016).

For further reading

Assembly of First Nations. "Honoring Earth." http://www.afn.ca/honoring-earth/

Battiste, M. "You can't be the global doctor if you're the colonial disease." In P. Tripp & L. Muzzin, eds., *Teaching as Activism*. Montreal: McGill Queen's U P, 2005. 121-133.

Bouchier, Nancy B., and Ken Cruikshank. *The People and the Bay: A Social and Environmental History of Hamilton Harbour*. UBC Press, rpt 2016.

Bramadat, Paul, and David Seljak. *Christianity and Ethnicity in Canada*. U of Toronto P, 2008.

Bumsted, J. M. *The Peoples of Canada: A Pre-Confederation History*. 4th ed. Oxford U P, 2014.

Coleman, Daniel. *Yardwork: A Biography of an Urban Place*. James Street North Books, 2017.

Fong, Eric, ed. *Inside the Mosaic*. U of Toronto P, 2006.

Hill, Daniel G. *The Freedom Seekers: Blacks in Early Canada*. Book Society of Canada, 1992.

Hill, Susan M. *The Clay We Are Made Of: Haudenosaunee Land Tenure on the Grand River*. U of Manitoba P, 2017.

Oakville Historical Society. *The History of the Mississaugas of the New Credit First Nation*. https://www.oakvillehistory.org/uploads/2/8/5/1/28516379/the-history-of-mncfn-final.pdf

O'Hara, Paul. *A Trail Called Home: Tree Stories from the Golden Horseshoe*. Dundurn P, 2019

Rogers, E., and D. Smith. *Aboriginal Ontario: A History of the First Nations*. Dundurn P, 1994

Root, Emily. "This Land is Our Land? This Land is Your Land: The Decolonizing Journeys of White Outdoor Environmental Educators." *Canadian Journal of Environmental Education*, 15, 2010. 103-119.

Schmalz, Peter S. *The Ojibwa of Southern Ontario*. U of Toronto P, 1991.

Shadd, Adrienne. *The Journey from Tollgate to Parkway: African Canadians in Hamilton*. Dundurn P, 2010.

Steinauer-Scudder, Chelsea. "Hallowed Ground: A Profile of Martin Palmer." *Emergence Magazine*, April 28, 2019. https://emergencemagazine.org/story/hallowed-ground/

Webber, L.R., and D. W. Hoffman. *Origin, Classification and Use of Ontario Soils.* U of Guelph, 1967.

Wybenga, Darin P. "Mississaugas of the Credit First Nation." *The Canadian Encyclopedia* Sept. 21, 2022. https://thecanadianencyclopedia.ca/en/article/mississaugas-of-the-credit-first-nation

--- & Kaytee Dalton. *Mississaugas of the New Credit First Nation, Past & Present.* MNCFN, 2018. https://mncfn.ca/wpcontent/uploads/2018/10/MississaugasoftheNewCreditFirstNation-PastPresentBooklets-PROOFv4-1.pdf

Winks, Robin. *The Blacks in Canada: A History*. McGill-Queen's U P, 1997.

Wood, J. David. M*aking Ontario: Agricultural Colonization and Landscape Recreation Before the Railway.* McGill-Queen's U P, 2000.

POEMS IN PLACE

LAND

"Restoring land without restoring relationship is an empty exercise. It is relationship that will endure and relationship that will sustain the restored land. Therefore, reconnecting people and the landscape is as essential as re-establishing proper hydrology or cleaning up contaminants. It is medicine for the earth."

—**Robin Wall Kimmerer**, *Braiding Sweetgrass* [29]

[29] Excerpt from "The Sacred and the Superfund" from *Braiding Sweetgrass: Indigenous Wisdom, Scientific Knowledge and the Teachings of Plants*. Copyright © 2013, 2015 by Robin Wall Kimmerer. Reprinted with the permission of The Permissions Company, LLC on behalf of Milkweed Editions, milkweed.org.

Deeds [30]

Long line of sour-faced Loyalist leeches
bleeding bunting, solemnly landed
on cold crown land writ on sacred native soil
hatchet buried like burdock birthing
sprawled roots of resentment.

Plowing hymn stave furrows over the brow
of the landscape. Hair raised daguerreotypes
silvering over seeded hopes
praying on god-fear
wresting native land.

Felled and burnt, savagely scavenged
carved the topsoil skin into
ditches and corduroy scars
over the sacred backs to claim
with a structure only to cough blood,

---

[30] Author's note: "My poems for this anthology come from a place of ambivalence about my family history. Before she died my mother and her cousin made a booklet with details of the family history. Her family came to Canada as U.E.L.s in 1799. Laurence and Suzannah were granted land in Palermo and had 11 children. Laurence left Suzannah alone to fight in the War of 1812. Two of their sons founded towns. One founded Hagersville and the other, my ancestor, founded Middleport. He was given a land grant along the Grand River, which, by Treaty rights, was native land. His wife Jerusha Currie Hager had 14 children. Her husband died at 43. She was pregnant. Her oldest son was killed three months later in a logging accident. The baby died within seven months. Their children attended the native school. One of the children, Emma, is said to have been in a class with Pauline Johnson. Their son had James, who in turn had Elmer, who became my mother's father.

"My mother was very sympathetic to the native situation and was somewhat ashamed of her history. She felt there were some redeeming qualities in the character of Jerusha, who could not have managed without the help of her native neighbours. Her husband and sons were the only non-native people buried in the native cemetery. They now rest in the brambles beside it. My pieces reflect on my similar feelings about the stories."

[Elizabeth Tessier's second poem in this anthology, "Looming," is in the "Farming and Gardening" section.]

die and lie sewn like a wry weed
on foreign soil
choking out the native life,
boring holes in the boreal
forest with Protestant fervor.

Elizabeth Tessier

Welcome to My Home

Cedar, Sweetgrass, Sumac.
Barefoot in the forests of Stoney Creek,
opening new leaves, taking a peek,
thanking Creator and the Land for medicines:
harmony guides us with four directions.

At the bottom of Bay Street,
I honour the water, for I am her daughter.
She glistens and speaks,
the wise listen—and peek

as she births the beauty, the leaves of the trees,
the beauty of life, the natural streaks
of red, green and blue. Thought up
the land, sky, and full forest in view.

These trails I have walked, all along this land,
for I am Metis, running through harbour's sands,
listening to the birds, taking time to learn
rebirth causes the Earth.

I am simply a part of Her and Him:
I look at Moons and Stars when Sun
is dim. I wake and run, to witness leaves with dew
I rise with Sun, and watch
my manifest dreams come true.

Dear reader, like you I am hue-man too.
I have faith when all the grids open
I'll know what to do. Listen
closely to the raven birds
and the sheep's leather, cow herds

for on the earth, they speak,
even when times are deep.
They know as much and more than I,
and they know what to say when I rest to cry.

Arwen Roussell

Pray the Land

Loyola House, Guelph

Pray the land was what they counselled us,
a sentence syntactically, semantically wrong
to my ears. I set out over a landscape carved

by tractor tracks, past dark berries, red-
winged blackbirds, bee hives, along wood fences.
When had I last crossed a stile? Walking, I

discovered that I was a stranger to the land,
impermeable, it seemed, to the aura of the rural.
I was here alone beneath an entire sky.

I had come to risk days uncrowded by speech,
days that cocked my ear toward the sacred,
and I was in a sudden unborderedness of space.

I listened but found that the land had no voice,
only an inertness that mirrored my own.
I continued to attempt to pray with my feet,

to pray with my legs as I rose over the hills.
And quietly, perhaps shyly, something lifted itself,
tentatively offered itself to hearing—

it was of the depth and not the miraculous;
it was the ordinary revelation of the world.
It was as if I were that ancient a creature,

were someone older, ancestral, primordial,
of a lineage continuing, uninterrupted, in this walking.
And now the fist of what I had been

relaxed. I yielded to some easing of thought,
some loosening that let compressed years expand,
and I was strangely bared to listening,

here where I met the largesse of the world.
I might say it was a sacrament of being landed,
that I was where the sun earthed its warmth.

It was land that could be companion of my days,
land the one I was here to attend to,
the one I was here simply to attend.

Brian Day

Ancestor Song

Do you remember, you lived in a cave
You thought you knew the world
Its crevices and its curves
Do you remember, learning of the roof
Growing little girl, swiftly flying bird

Do you remember, discovering your voice
Hollow-bellied drum
Winding on your tongue tongue tongue
Do you remember, turning breath into sound
A litany of tones, melodies your own

Oh how sound echoes, waves off 'a walls
Never was a cage, was holding empty stage
Oh the earth glorious, oh the earth a symphony, a chorus
Listening the land, answer bouncing back

Do you remember, feeling your first ever breeze
Led you to a door, unknown to you before
Do you remember, the blinding of the sun
Expanding of the sky, opening your eyes
Be sure to remember, after this life
When body turns to earth, melodies survive
Listen, have you heard, inside you is a bird
Remember, carry on, ancestor song

Janice Jo Lee

Hilton Falls

The thing about fossils, says my brother,
is the way they blur the line between flesh
and stone. We're picking our way
along the muddy path toward the falls.
Water murmurs in our ears.
We stoop to examine the rocks,
check smooth surfaces for
a stamp of something once living:
patterns, textures, parallel lines;
fragments of shell; a tracing
that might be a leaf print.
We sift slowly through flakes of shale,
turn over fist-sized chunks.

I think I've found one.
My brother peers at it. *Could be a trilobite.*
Brachiopod, maybe. Hard to tell.
Before he can pocket the stone I take it back.
I hold it lightly as we walk
and slide my thumb along its tiny grooves.

Joanne Epp

All We Know of Angels

Dear God the very boulders are awake,
the mists levitate off the
river, the morning rises, the very

river turns in its bed
and we earnest every eager
man-jack of us dogbodies

shake our hides
from under the great woven wings
of the dog-angel dark

and slew forth
sniffing and sleuthing
for a trace of the great passing or pausing

of your jeezly footsteps
on the nap of the dewlapped
love'sbodied earth:

earthlings. Missionaries in reverse.
Into the hinterlands we hurtle to have your
missives cackle and guffaw

about our buzzing ears, fly-talk
and bee-talk and cricket mission memos
and the dew, the pearly

everlasting, drench-wetting
us to the breeks so we know we've been.
We were. We went. We've come to say:

All I know of angels
    is this unsullied dawn at the start of things
        here in Harm's Way, this temple-

busting whitebreak
    that weans the sleeper
        from his dark fit and flat out

into the newness of the unshaven day,
    this charge of the light brigade, this christly
        gallivanting of wings in time

with four legs at concert pitch as the wind
    riffles the score on a thousand leaves times ten
        thousand and last night's electric

attention calms
    to this conducted windrowed
        morning's scattered munificence,

a diaspora of wings,
    wanton with appearances,
        hiding made visible.

Mia Anderson

Reclamation

He was the first to build a picture window
shear off trees
leaving the tangling roots.
He trimmed the greening earth
and ferreted out weeds
with methodical madness.
The wire-worms slipped deeper down their black holes.

Some white days the lake became sky
and his world stopped at the cliff edge.
The water sucked sand
from under his feet
stole beneath the slope
cracked the surface
and a piece of his world was space.

On limpid winter nights
he slid down the ice banks
while the swells slapped below
like a father admonishing an infant.
What stars,
silent eyes in a midnight forest,
plotted his possibilities?

He moved his chair to the centre of the room
when the wave gathered
like legions on the horizon line
rolling high over the water
a raw emerald curl
swallowing beach and cliff
crashed upon the window

and receded
dropping grey-white mountains on his lawn.
The second ice-blue force
smashed the glass
and spent its last upon his eyes.
Quiescent
he waited for the ice to come.

David Haskins

Li, The Clinging, Fire[31]

Pacific storms strip sand from beaches, expose a shore
of carved, conglomerate shelves. Highrises and city sidewalks
are built upon the compacting weight of shell middens

and plumes of hot, buoyant rock rising from earth's molten core.
Semis roll down the 401 alongside green fields, where cows graze.
The day I got out of my car to be near them, inhale their Jersey breath.

Cornelia Hoogland

31 Author's note: "From *Cosmic Bowling*, which is a conversation between a poet and a sculptor (Ted Goodden), triangulated through the ancient book of wisdom, the I Ching—a compendium of Taoist, Buddhist and Confucian thought. The triangulation complicates the present moment both on and off the page, on freeways and in the fields around us." For a short video promoting *Cosmic Bowling*, see https://www.youtube.com/watch?v=9kL9XpU2Pqs

A French-Canadian, but not really, moves to Hamilton

This is Hamilton, or so I have been told
maximizing economic growth
minimizing environmental damage
this conundrum of a place is unsettling, a settler
am I a settler to Hamilton? a transplanted body
in pursuit of knowledge under the watchful
eye of the Dundas Marsh and Burlington Bay,
Steel City now haunts me.

Steel City, cold and from the earth
but not really of the earth
I am talking about me, I am not
from this world of salmon and waterfalls,
living on borrowed time and queer lands,
tucked away behind a MacBook screen
trapped in between discourses of urgency and joy,
economies of gratitude and spite.

What is my experience with the land?
Who is Hamilton to me? How is it?
How is it mind, body, emotion, spirit?
Is there animacy hidden away in the smog
bursting forth from the bellies of timeless plants
thriving on the earth of the manufacturing district
a microcosm, and gifts of subsistence for who?
Offerings once steeped in the human

abundances of sweat and blood, cars, churches,
trails, trains, trees, a lake that permitted
a people to settle indefinitely.
This WAS a working-class city,
as if somehow the work is done,

as if I am not here, now, somewhere, trying
to come to terms with the land in industrial country,
to become fluent in nature, in reciprocity.
I want to give Hamilton what it does not offer me.

Linzey Corridon

Escarpment (Autumn)

Meanwhile the areola continues, a lateral grey endosquirrel down superior ambiance
GLO frain to the distalwolf, a thoracic minksong down and down the porcupine of
VENTRA tolight. Eastern Occipital wood. Woodchuck proximal. Great shrew of red
BAT MEAD wbright. Deer cooling against the cranial vole. The auricle inferior
APPREHEND the coyotoid awakening. Who played only what beaver chose, who chose
ONLY TO PLA "fovea muskrat fovea down." A dorsal sparrow emptied. The ruby short-
TAILED LUMBA f shoppingcart racoonoplasty. The pine vole's silverhaired kingfisher
PERCEIVES A NOR Ay rat of seminiferous stickleback. Time's flying needleminer. It
ISN'T A HORSEN Tosilver, wisenheimer. There weren't birch skeletonizers to
BULLRUSH DELTOI duskbat hiss. At the brush wolf. When they were mink. The
HUMANS WERE HAR glossy woodland. The children asleep on the dendrite swallow
WITH THE MOTOR W ral bellybreath the ornamental swan of the pelvis. The
SPIDER'S PRIVATE LIF ows animating a boxelder. "Never avert your eyes." (Pine
SPITTLEBUG.) THE ANTH ne writing of light, a flocking of swallows.
MORE THAN MAGNOLIA, CREP missed. The white bushes especially.
AGAINST UNDIFFERENTIATED D IT IS like night. Lustrous ratclever clavicle.
THE FLEXING VESPER BLUET. PRING er at the shoulder is nightgown
CEPHALON. ADMIT A COMMON HOPTRE striation. an exomouth cloud. Then
VESTIBULAR MOON IN THE FORKTAIL POS m, amber-winged bagplastic pleura
GIVES MUDPUPPY BLUE-BEECH SQUIRR ectomy. mockorange leafminer.
AGONISTIC KENTUCKY DORSAL. BLACK OAK byspot floats gluteal over mute
TRUMPETER'S HIGH CEILING. BEYOND THE U BILical owl, the landclaims
SATURATE ADRENAL DOLLAR LEVELS OF AB ting salamander. Illuminating
GREBE AND ARROWHEAD SPIKETAIL. THE OV swan of the moon. Astonishing
OUR EARTHLINESS. I WAS THERE. SO THE WHIT hroated lamplight needs radiant
WAXWING. RACKET-TAILED EMERALD. DUSKY ubtail. Spatterdock darner. Pass
WITH CARE. COOTES. STERNAL ESCARPMENT. oud children. Cootes. Refrain:
THE EARLY MEDIOLATERAL BUTTERCUP BLIN he river. with a mirror. Then
PERIWINKLE COCCYX OVER THE DARKENED C ian room. Puts a vagabound
STONECAT ON ITS SIGHTLESS FACE. MOONEYES mic shiner for this, trifathead
CHECKERSPOT FOR THAT. WE CALL IT OPERA disease. Then leave them there.
THE QUILLGREY VENTRALMARSH OF THE RA OO dlebags handspring
THE LATERAL HILLS. BORN WITH HAIRSTREAKS AND BLUE. MED ERAL
THE ROAD'S DENIAL. THEY WOULD HAVE BEEN BLUE—THE EYES—BLUE
AS DITCH. NOW WE SEE FARTHER WOLF AND FARTHER DISTALWOLF STILL
LIGHT WAS EXPECTED TO BE VISIBLE AND IT WAS GROPING AROUND THE
SLEEPING BROOK IN OUR SQUIRRELGOWNS VENTRAL FROG OF THE
UNSEEN BREATHDARK SPARROW FILLS EVERY VACANCY THORACIC
FIREFLIES MAKES A LEFT OVER THE CENTRAL MUDMINNOW. ELBOW
DEER A LITTLE PAST THE BLACK SPRUCE OF STARS. SUDDENLY THE
FEELING OF GREAT CLOUDYWING SKIPPERS. A DELIRIOUS BRILLIANCE.
THE YELLOW BIRCH. ITS UNTAMABLE EYES IN THE NIGHT. AGAIN GREAT
SHREW OF RED BAT MEADOWBRIGHT. EASTERN OCCIPITAL WOOD.
WOODCHUCK PROXIMAL. IT USED TO BE SO PRETTY HERE. AND IT IS. ~~~

Gary Barwin

Oh, Mother Earth

Chorus: *Oh, Mother Earth, we are your children—*
Trees an' people an' field an' stream:
Oh, Mother Earth, we are your children—
We want to thank you, we want to dream!
Expediency lives in our hearts:
Just for a dollar, just for a buck
We rip off tomorrow and sell off today—
What makes us think we won't have to pay?
Chorus

The trees give their lives
to unmask people's greed:
People and trees are all family—
We're killing this planet by hating our mother.
Chorus

How can I be still and keep my mouth shut?
The air is polluted, the water is too.
Our time may be borrowed, our time may be through—
We're killing our future by hating our mother.
Chorus

My cry is a warning the chaos is near,
We're killing our future by bowing to fear.
Can you hear me, Mother Earth? The love in my heart?
My laughter is hidden, my tears ever flow.
Chorus

Our hearts they are breaking and need to be filled—
The trees are our family and mustn't be killed.
Chorus: *Oh, Mother Earth, we are your children—*
Trees an' people an' field an' stream:
Oh, Mother Earth, we are your children—
We need to thank you, we need to dream!

Honey Novick

Mother Earth

I was out in the field, firing off orders of
what was to be done
When a man appeared from behind the
glare of the sun
He asked me by what I right I claim this land
So I took out the paper and placed it in his hand
This gives me the right to do as I please
I own the dirt, I own the trees

This land provides me with economic prosperity
When I look upon this land it is money
as far as the eye can see

The old man looked at me with the saddest eyes
Bent and picked up a handful of dirt
and said, you actually believe those lies

In my hand I hold all that you were, are,
and will ever be
You may be able to lie to yourself but not to me
This gave life to you and me
And provided for everything you have and
everything you see

This is the reason for our birth
And the reason my people call this land
Mother Earth

The Earth gave you life and provided the
necessities as you grew
The Earth nurtures you and will one day reclaim you

Maybe the courts will accept that paper as true
But we both know who owns who.

Gimaa (Chief) R. Stacey Laforme

WATER

"*Daylighting* is the term used when buried creeks are freed to run in the open again. If the land is alive and thinking, then listening to and engaging with these living streams could help us retune our relationship with this place. By the song of its strings, we may be healed."

—**John Terpstra**, *Daylighting Chedoke* [32]

[32] John Terpstra, *Daylighting Chedoke: Exploring Hamilton's Hidden Creek* (James Street North Books, 2018).

Giants

There used to be giants,
and they loved it here. They'd sit
their giant hinds in a row along the top edge
of the escarpment, and pick at the loose rock
with their hands or their feet, then throw or skip
the smoothest stones across the bay, to see who could land one
on the sandstrip, three miles away;

or they'd spring themselves off the scarp top
like you would off a low wall, and go running
all the way to the end of the sandbar,
and jump across the water to the other side,
or jump in, splashing and yelling up the ravines,
chasing each other's echoes.

This was only a few thousand years ago,
and the giants were still excited about the glaciers,
which were just leaving; about not having to wear
their coats all the time, and what
the ice and water had done, shaping and carving
this gentle, wild landscape!

They loved it here.

I'm telling you, they absolutely loved
every living minute here,

and they regretted ever having to leave.

John Terpstra

A Brief History of Water Falling

There's a single swan in Beverly swamp,
alien white,
one foot outstretched across its back,
one foot wading murky water,
suspended between sky and land,
bridging two worlds together,
equilibrium incarnated.

Here is a place where water falls
darker and denser inside the Armpit.
Rain inherits traces of the labor of the living,
family pools proliferate summers
littered with skin and dirt and foliage,
factories offer tributes to the heavens,
converting mineral extract to nimbostratus.

Here waterfalls are industrious,
collecting the unrest of homo sapiens
transformed into treasures 130 times over.
One hundred thirty bodies absolving us of history,
liquid beings who beg nothing in return,
only that we revere them
a little less artifice,
a little less of us in them.

We hide from the rain,
umbrellas keeping soiled droplets away.
We complain of residue on our cars,
our air conditioners carry the stench of toiling
on days when *la pluie* courts the city.

In every instance, water swells with history,
archiving our endeavours in river streams,
libraries of once disjointed lives rushing towards the bay
more lucid and lighter than we could ever imagine.

Linzey Corridon

City with a View

We are a city on the edge
and beyond. On the escarpment
one becomes a small child
lifted onto her father's shoulders
again, astonished at the sudden vistas.

Yet we dream of being
Toronto dreaming of being
New York. Erecting
brave new buildings
over derelict lots
we demolish old trees
and fountains.

We believe the lake
should be used and not seen.
Pool owners and cottagers,
we come to work every day
oblivious of the lake beside us,
the lake in our faucets.
This lake which we are
poisoning will poison us,
who so love being a city
that we have forgotten the earth,
except here and there:

here in the gardens
where memory sweetly lingers
to water our senses
and to pollinate light with colour,

and there on the edge
of the escarpment
where we are surprised again
every time
by where we are.

Bernadette Rule

Commencement for Cootes Paradise

1

Fish hovering above silt. Their mouths open, hoovering the almost dark.

10,000 Olympic-sized swimming pools. If humans are 60% water—heart 73%, lungs 83%—how many humans is that? Varicoloured humans reaching forward, displacing the river, swimming, floating in liquid sky.

Someone left a valve open.

They told us in science class: Love + Time = Death.

No, that was my Grade 9 girlfriend. Our world is sensation and memory, our 73% brains, our 31% bones.

Stellar nucleosynthesis resulting in the complex organic molecules necessary for life formed in the protoplanetary disk of dust grains surrounding the Sun before the formation of the Earth + energy = city counsellors.

24 billion gallons of sewage is what is going on inside of us, while 24 billion gallons of sewage is what we do on the outside. Or, according to David Kessler, grief.

Old David Foster Wallace fish: Morning, boys. How's the water?
Young David Foster Wallace fish: What the hell is water?

2

The moon fills bedrooms, kitchens, basements with its sliver, staircases slick with shine. 24 billion gallons of fish slide into our homes, our 73% brain a stippled perch spawning at night.

Here's the heart pumping under its sheath of shad.

Here's largemouth bass slithering upstream toward heart chambers. A thousand vena cava
tributaries, the watershed of our fist-size swims.

A valve releases fish and eels, frogs and water voles into our chests, our "forever" mudrooms and rec rooms. Here fish + eels + frogs + voles = 24 billion gallons of sewage and runoff.

A mouth a kind of valve, open—largemouthed, duckfaced—to the dark everywhere. Here our breathing strained through the weir of our teeth. How many breaths fill an Olympic pool? No. We breathe air, it's the gills of our grade 9 girlfriend where water fins.

City counsellors stock pockets with frogs, fish, eels, water voles, lift glasses from their civic desks, tip lakewater in. A sidereal biome. Removable. A hand's worth of pond or river. Shh, the susurration of rippling. Shh, the secrets held in a closed mouth, a net, a Celtic knot of fish.

What-the-hell water where fish glug and burble, tell-it-truth light slanted toward silt. What is river, is lake, is marsh, is Time + Death = Love.

My Grade 9 girlfriend and me on the shore of Cootes Paradise, human as driftwood, twig-sized toes sunk and wet in the near shore sandy muck, blood circulating under our high school skin as if across the upper city, combed by waterfalls, raked over escarpment cliffs, runnelling down rivers into a lake where our feet stand in the cool and, hands in each other's hands, we open our mouths to the dark, breathe stickleback, tadpole madtom, green sunfish, finescale dace, northern hognose sucker.

How much dark in a river, in a lake or marsh? How much light? Watershed of night, of day. Those with veins. Those without.

No, it wasn't my Grade 9 girlfriend. It wasn't me. We weren't looking at 24 billion gallons, its dark surface, 100 billion pounds of starlight gone. A nearly 100% full moon.

What + what = this? What + what is here to breathe the silt of this dark night?

Gary Barwin

The Expectant Lake

I don't believe that dolphins dared to swim
in canals in absence of gondolas
or that goats ventured into new grounds
to look through the windows of a house

in the spring the whole world huddled
inside to escape from the viral spread

I went for a walk at the Bayfront Park
where the year before a stench came up
out of the waters from phosphate-fed
blue-green toxic algae blooms

condominiums nearby held their noses
let summer sail pass like others before

I stood on the edge
pinched my skin
opened my eyes
to see
if there were dolphins
or humpback whales

Lake Ontario remained
expectant as goats
hoping for something else
instead of pollution or fantasy

Jennifer Tan

Somewhere, a Lake

As sun heals the surface of ice, I lose my footing
on Ramsay Lake. My heel pierces the thin crust and I
recollect the depths to which light can take me. That day

the lake, soft at the centre, a wedding cake with white
shavings. Shoe to snowshoe to snow, phase transitions, tight
mid-winter molecules. Simple steps inflate hours

breaths of air, voids of green, making escape a landscape.
Somewhere, a lake is always ice-free. Even then there's
a lake effect, that cold wind travelling across warm

water bodies, producing energy, reminding
me I know the fluid three feet beneath me better
by summer sun. Like that night I took out the canoe

lips and atmosphere swelling with heat, a full August
moon burning a hole in the blinds, as I paddled to
the middle, ever expanding but with the absence

of perfect circles. Afterthoughts, the echoes of loons
the chord indefinable since points of reference
are never safe. All potential instabilities.

Tracks of red fox, more evidence of indirection,
their graceful arcs vanish before the grey horizon
or underneath a few centimetres of falling.

New snow quiets everything except flashy lures for
walleye below, who find the human-sized holes, baited
to surrender themselves to what they truly believe

is the eye of spring. Night freezes only the slightest
of wounds. Every morning the path is once again mine
to forge or forsake. There's an end in sight, a shore, with
pain before dawn, love after light, an outing of ice.

Madhur Anand

Still of the Lake

Let the lake settle, be still, for sand pull on down
Dock the boats, reel in the rods, fish out what don't belong
Everything this body needs swirls within itself
Algae cells, coves and wells, blood, mud and shells

Skin of the surface permeable to light, to eyes, to sight
Bouncing off mirror scattering glance, a crystal, a prism, a dance
'Til flecks and specks relax, float low, slip curtain aside to show
Innervision, inventory, recovery, clarity

Still of the Lake, oh to see
Still of the lake, oh to breathe

Enveloped inside memories hide, far deep, 'neath scars of war
Cellar storage, treasure forage, rot and mould untold
What bits have sunk? Built up a trunk? Or gleaned away by stream
Go in, begin, search within, infer, discover, swim

Breach in the air, groove in the earth, fluid a pack intact
Waiting ready, cushioning, drizzle or hail or sleet
All shots are caught a yielding shield, cradled and held in field
Dip in with ease, wetted leave, filter to dry, a sieve

Still of the Lake, oh to see
Still of the lake, oh to breathe

Janice Jo Lee

Window to a Lake *(written in Burlington, Ontario)*

Reposed upon an armchair of a rock
taking stock through window to lake staring
perusing a departing spring evening's view
chewing on a thought or few
raking feelings for clarity's sake
I pursue serenity within soul-ache
rummage remnants of a done day
reminiscing on a land faraway

But beauty nearby rivets my itinerant eye
a spectacular ocular array adorns the dusky bay
fishing boats, drifting, sway
splashing waves flash unsalted spray
grey, smoky, sky patrolled by birds of prey
ducks and swans still dare to cavort and play
and somehow, along the way
softly, yet suddenly

Poetry's epiphany reveals to me
that the lake's landlocked captivity
might make it sometimes wish to be an open sea

Klyde Broox

Looking Out

It has been said that a pilgrim becomes addicted to the horizon
that semi-mythical distance we all know we can
never get to
that line we can never cross.

Many people make a pilgrimage to a great lake in summer.

The man who every day wears dark clothing in this heat,
has he come to absorb through his eyes and his ears
the rhythm of grief—
whelm of engulfment
the reliable wane?

The woman in the straw hat who sits on the grey beach
every morning looking out.
Perhaps she's allowing
the trance of just being
to subsume her.

What happens when you spend time
on the edge
of such power, such beauty, such
possibility?

The longer I stand looking out, the smaller I become.

This morning, an expanding light that begins on the horizon,
Bright and wide as our vision, coming toward us across the big water.

Toward us or perhaps for us.

A light that makes you understand why
they were once *sore afraid.*

Marilyn Gear Pilling

Breakwater

Pipe-staked, dynamite-stuffed limestone, blasted slabs
of fossil rock, time-press of ancient seas, sediments
snail into shellish shapes, creature tracks like hieroglyphics,
the cut rock—scooped and horse-carted out—
slowly, the hole fills … and up like an escaping creature,

a liquid cemetery air sac for abandoned machinery.
Hoofprints, bootprints dissolve to fish
inside the growing fluid. Water, now free to roam, softens
walls of its open-air cage, whitecapped, flat, cottonseed-coated,
leafed, sun-loved or winter-taken, the wait for forms to crawl out.

Catherine Graham

The Paris Raceway

... allotting to them for that purpose
six miles deep from each side of the river ...
to which them and their posterity are to enjoy for ever.
(Haldimand Proclamation, 1794)

Most every day we visit the river
walk down to hear its chattering, listen
how this time the story is different again
see what boulders are out in the air of it,
if an eagle is in the far cottonwood, or if
an osprey or three will careen this way.

Out back of our place, purchased fair and square,
the yard eventually wanders to a berm
of shallowly buried, broken down red bricks
gathered up in every tree's roots, the crumbs of it
floods the soil here. And further down,
down to the edge, the river shallow,
a boneyard of swept cobblestones and boulders
crossable on foot, rolling over
and over into a river never at rest.
Each day we visit her, to hear the chortling
see the rise and fall, catch her resilient spirit.

It's easy to wonder why the founders bothered here
just below the new Paris where the Grand widens
and flattens out, not even decent for a canoe
to paddle through. Yet in the 1850s a raceway was built
right where our property ends. The river's edge
dredged into a channel, the shore's footing
secured with milled planking and brickwork,

where horses dragged large boats upstream
into the village with all manner of goods,
and back out full of gypsum for the world.

The river's edge, where the original tribes
had always waded, Iroquois and Wyandot,
the deer plentiful, turkeys and beaver, trout
turning over and over in the currents. This land
taken by foreigners then settled by treaty,
given to six other tribes from elsewhere—
promised the finger lakes but gifted the long valley.
Within a decade most of the valley handed back
by sale and leases, dishonourable dealings.

I keep digging up bricks, broken chunks and red dust
wonder when I'll ever find arrowheads, beading
or preserved ancient tools in this boneyard
of swept cobblestone and boulders,
crossable here, on foot, rolling over
and over into a river shallow, but never at rest.
And each day we visit her, to hear the chittering,
see the rise and fall, catch her out in the air of it.

Mark Kempf

A Feminist Guide to Reservoirs

You want to, but can't
scream at how
we're hated. But you

recall that herons stand
all day in retention
ponds, keep their distance

from other herons.
It is not moot to say
those herons know

what you're missing.
You have long
suspected capitalism hates

women and geese crave
stormwater
and gender parity.

You walk how you can when you
walk by the reservoir.
Occupy everything Dionne Brand said

and the gymnasium of students
rose as one body
to their feet, roaring, and

you thought you had made it,
battered but alive,
to the future. The river

is charged with all the artificial
sweeteners that pass
unaltered through our bodies,

down the sewers and into the river,
molecules of Coke
slipping down the geological

staircase into Lake Erie, Haldimand
Tract, six miles on
both sides of the river, Six Nations

land, and every white person
you know acts
so surprised. *Oh, I didn't*

know. One in three
women will
be sexually assaulted.

I was never taught that.
No one is, until
you are. A creek can

whisper through a city,
a rumour of water
that is water. You cannot

get your breath. Someone
spray-paints
I Am Broken on the bunker

over the culvert where
you watch mallards
emerge like a magic

act. You're not, or not
any more
than usual. The gates

open and the creek
roars down from where
it's been reserved,

disguised as a pond all
summer, held back
like a sneeze.

This is not moot,
not meant
to please.

Tanis MacDonald

Some Grand River Blues[33]

Look. The land ends up
in stubble every
October. The sky
today may feel as

empty. But just be
like the river—bend
and reflect it. Those
blues already show

through the skin inside
your elbow—and flow
back to the heart. Why
let a few passing

Canada geese up
set you? Just remind
yourself how the land
also renews. Don't

despair just because
they're already too
high to hear. Your heart
started beating with

their wings the moment
you got sight of them
--but that's no reason
to fear it will still

---

[33] This poem is recorded on CD at *Range River Poems*, by Daniel David Moses, with music by David Deleary (2009).

when they disappear.
Look away now. Let
loose. See? The river's
bending like a bruise.

Daniel David Moses

Eye of the Farm

In the depths of the valley
between the two farms
where willows overhung
water, where dragonflies
flittered and folded
where the creek bulged round,
was the swimming hole.
Above it, the log that allowed
us to cross or to lie
full length on its heat.
If ever there was a little heaven
for my brother and me
this was it.
Afternoons as long as a summer,
sun-warmed water shimmer
mirrored trees, long strands
of willow, everything imagined
as part of another world
we alone knew. Unique
smell of creek life
that stayed in our hair,
water spiders, crayfish
stonefish, families of leaves
that floated from upstream
passed beneath our log and
travelled on once we had
stopped them, warmed them
on the log, heard their stories
told them ours.
In the creek, the large flat stone
from which we launched ourselves
into water that allowed us
to enter its being, and belong.

Marilyn Gear Pilling

TREES

"Trees are the great storytellers of the landscape, looking glasses into the past. … They speak of natural history, First Nations history, and colonial history. Trees also speak of power and spirit. Through a greater understanding of trees, we can tap into that power and spirit and become more rooted to the land beneath our feet, and our place in it."
—**Paul O'Hara**, *A Trail Called Home*[34]

[34] Paul O'Hara, *A Trail Called Home: Tree Stories from the Golden Horseshoe* (Toronto: Dundurn P, 2019), p. 56. See too Paul O'Hara's photo website at atrailcalledhome.ca

Woodland Occupation of North Dumfries Township

Among the Chippewa
young hickory   basswood or elm
some sought ironwood because it bends easily when green
or tamarack

and the Hurons preferred
cedar bark for roofing
harvested in spring when the sap was running and flats from elm
yellow birch   chestnut   oak   pine   black ash or hemlock
peeled off the living trees

Among the Potawatomi
elm bark
or slippery elm

Among the Algonquin
the bark of walnut trees   which is wondrous tough
lashed together with pliable strips of fresh white oak
or inner green basswood made into cordage

The Iroquoians preferred
the elm   to chestnut   hemlock   basswood or ash
for sheathing their longhouses

Among the Winnebago
walls were of plaited cedar bark
or black ash bark   or birch was used
about a yard square sewn together
with spruce root

And all made
watertight with spruce gum caulking

Karen Houle

eastern white cedar

the cedar prepares the body
no fact or reason, no rational act

but ceremony, washing, love, liturgy
reminiscence, one cold body
near another

the cedar sits at the bedside
in the night, it sleeps and
its branches pump in breathbeats

all its hours are a beating dream

the cedar takes your hand
moves you from one indistinguishable
work of labour to another.

Anna Bowen

Forest Songs

Wind twirls and whistles
        in fir and pine
Carrying cool whispers up
        to those who listen
Giants with skin of bark
        arms of poplar reach,
scratching old grandfather tree's backside
        their toes under mossy fields
wiggle and touch
        warning when birds swoop in
gathering on branches
        amassing across limbs.

Suddenly a choir
erupting jubilant,
        unbroken notes, harmoniously
floating up to the
        rain makers and star holders
who grasp onto them,
        transforming songs into tears.

Corri Daniels

Autumn Reverie

Crisp dampness and a hint of frost,
the first fallen top the undergrowth
become one in step and sound.
Others stay behind, clutch
the branches afraid to drop off
the face of the earth.
What happens next
when you've spent your life
feeding the large other and the community?
What follows is a silent departure.
The forgotten wait to fall apart:
sponginess of first decay,
crackle as skins fall off,
reveal a tracery of bones.

Elizabeth McCallister

Fossil wood

Hemlocks do not now form a part of the European forests, but fossil hemlock wood has been discovered in various sections of that continent. [35]

crack open one of my bones and read the rings—summers of sugared
cold coffee, elixirs, sweat, the air
hanging heavy with lilac, lavender, lemon balm, red apple blossom
the cinnamon-red marrow, the grey-purple of organ meat

read the air in the inner bark, particles of chipboard and dust,
the glass factory and the transport trucks, the evaporation of sidewalk rivulets
tobacco, mullein, rose petals, colt's foot, trace your finger along the inhale

the eastern hemlock ranges from Cape Breton Island westward to Lake Superior
hops in the van after summer exams, rides west, sleeps through the stop
for McDonald's breakfast sandwiches, would have rolled her eyes

holds thread-like stems together with tolerance, with flattened cross-sections
is fertile only in the middle scales, keeps it to herself, whispers it only
to the leading shoot, hides it from woody projections

in the fossil wood a breath exhales, meeting the bone breath
the broth of stories simmered and lost across continents
this hemlock wood snaps, exposes its rings, meets my own
our fossil wood lies side by side, hums a single note of water.

Anna Bowen

---

[35] *Native Trees of Canada*, 5th edition (Department of Northern Affairs and National Resources, Forestry Branch: Ottawa, 1956) p.48. [Author's note.]

Place

A tree, when it first begins to shoot from the ground, immediately senses the potential lying within that one location and is persuaded to stay.

By never moving from its original location a tree is in the unique position of learning all there is to know about that one particular spot: the composition of earth, the characteristic of each wind, the inquisition of water, both above ground and under, the traffic of animals, humans, and more—most, or all, of which is modified, or determined, by its presence.

Every tree therefore is a specialist, the one expert in its own self-defined field, and cannot be made redundant.

John Terpstra

How to Get Lost in Your Backyard

When emerald ash borers move lock, stock, and wriggling barrel into the backyard tree, the whole yard tips off-balance. The golden giant is gutted from the inside. Ashes don't go to ashes, but to pulp. The day the crew comes to cut her down and grind her stump, you are away pushing paper around your desk. You come home to a ghost tree. Without the wooden lodestar, the sky flips beneath your feet when you stand in the yard; its main mast gone, the whole yard yaws. You plant your feet where her trunk stood and reach up. The yard rocks, then settles. From here in Ontario with your arms raised you can see the big poplar on the corner, hear it soughing a prairie evening. The cedars lean hard to the left and the susans turn their single black eyes. You could stand here forever, riding the worldtide in a flannel shirt, but a porcupine ambles out of the crawlspace behind the shed. You drop your arms and the porcupine winks out like a comet. You're here again.

Tanis MacDonald

Talk of Trees

I sit in the city park late in the day
and alone with autumn
watching the poplars
spin their yellow leaves
in the wind
they rattle there in the thousands
and go still, rattle and go still
as heaven darkens down
like the dimming to grey of a huge blue-roofed room
and Bruce comes by
walking his small dog
and we talk of these particular trees
how important simplicities
have become
as we age in the sound of the wind
with its voice of evening
fathering the far edges of everything
like the whispering secrets
of lost gods
who cannot find the words
for where they are in the world

and the leaves twist and turn
like the fixing of time
to an imprecision
with a windy aspiration of shadow say

and I am arriving at the true interior quality of light
where it touches the darkness of the heart
like memory and dream
and Bruce asks me, "will you write of this"
and I say, "no, not of this"

John B. Lee

The Highway that Became a Footpath

after the other side won the civic election

And I saw a new heaven and a new earth,
for the first heaven and the first earth had passed away,
and I saw the holy city, coming down out of heaven,
and the holy raving protester who climbed into a tree
to resist the building of the last highway
was still in among the leaves,
but the tree had grown much taller,
and the protester had been living up there for such a long time,
not alone, that several generations of protesters now populated the canopy,
freely trafficking the branches of their swaying neighbourhoods,
as the six-lane highway
wound between the trunks below
as wide only as a footpath,
a red-dirt earthway busy with pedestrians.
And the highway-that-became-a-footpath
led past the longhouse raised
during the same resistance, down in the valley,
for it still existed (both longhouse and valley existed still)
and other longhouses,
which were standing at that location several centuries earlier,
had re-materialized, their hearth-fires
burning still; an entire village, thriving
beside the hallowed creek that ran through the east end of the city.
And I saw the trees that formed the longhouse walls
take root, and continue to grow,
forty-thousand times forty-thousand,
their canopy providing all the roof
that the people needed.
And from a privileged perch at the top of the escarpment,
watching as the new city came down out of heaven,
it was clear that the leaves of those trees
were for the healing of the community.

John Terpstra

Red Hill Chainsaw Massacre

(Requiem for Red Hill Valley, Hamilton, Ontario)

Red Hill chainsaw massacre
Red Hill chainsaw massacre
Roaring steel teeth of chainsaw
Snake-oiled pipelines of white people law
Lip service to the Iroquois
Red Hill chainsaw massacre
Red Hill chainsaw massacre

Arrest demonstrators, sue protesters
Police protection for bulldozers
Cut down forty-four thousand trees
Pass me a gas mask please!
Red Hill chainsaw massacre
Red Hill chainsaw massacre
No more peace in the valley
"Indian" Removal Policy
Pave the way for catastrophe
Red Hill chainsaw massacre
Red Hill chainsaw massacre
Scarred escarpment face
Botanical beauty laid waste
Desecrated tribal sites
Denial of earlier peoples' rights
Red Hill chainsaw massacre
Red Hill chainsaw massacre
Media bought and paid for
Democracy, a spectator
Distorted common opinion
Twisted arms of objection
Election as selection
Expressway to further pollution
Red Hill chainsaw massacre

Red Hill chainsaw massacre
Swapping oxygen for monoxide
Surely seems like collective suicide
Red Hill chainsaw massacre
Red Hill chainsaw massacre

Development of ecological deficit
Tomorrow does not deserve it

Klyde Broox

O Emmanuel

If it weren't a lion it could be a tree:
the very paradigm of immanence. Cut out for the role.
Not Song of the Rood but roots long in the bog and scree
of the mother-lode, living and breathing the whole

same stuff, the whole same non-negotiables as we.
You could ride it like a lion, astride its bole,
and be as winged as Gregory of Nyssa could be
just standing still. Now *that's* speed! Now *that's* fall-

ing upwards, that's grace, that's tree—tree's wisdom whispered
with each plebiscite of wind, its stylus light's green persuasion,
its theology water, its codex bedrock Precambrian shield.
No fight. No flight. Be clear *(pause)*: it will yield.
It will not (you'd rather otherwise) resist invasion,

stability and constancy preclude.
The tree was cut short: an interlude.

Stay with the interlude: step in under the shadow of its wings,
its boughs. There, be near what has come very near to things.

Mia Anderson

Mushquoteh

After conversation with environmentalist J. Johnson
"Mushquoteh" (Ojibwe):"place where deer come to feed"

Homesick, feeling the need of the familiar,
European colonists brought the broad-leaf
green maple tree to live in the northern
new world, replacing
the Indigenous red maple.

Audacious, tall, strong
sun-stretched branches growing
plentiful foliage outward, while
sinewy roots encroach deep, deeper
proclaiming its new home, destroying
an existing ecosystem.

This green umbrella shade is
so daunting, no sunshine could nurture
anything underneath—obliterating
the five-needle cluster eastern pine
of the five Iroquois nations.

Symbol of colonization, the
Norway maple spread, conquered,
adapted to this land, but
is not suited—now being
cut down and culled.

Mighty, audacious, conquering
like a land baron, maybe the
Norway maple is a new metaphor
for decolonization.

Honey Novick

BIRDS

Strange black and princely pirates of the skies,
Would that your wind-tossed travels I could know!
Would that my soul could see, and seeing, rise
To unrestricted life where ebb and flow
Of Nature's pulse would constitute a wider life below!
—E. Pauline Johnson (Tekahionwake)
"The Flight of the Crows"

Crow Out Early

The only one who speaks to this long rain
is that crow sitting on a pole like old
Raven, spitting out caws in pairs. He got
out of dreams on this wrong side of the bay.

Over there a foghorn makes a four-note
effort Crow can't comprehend. It's not like
even the loudest moans of his friends who
keep asleep, their effort to ignore how

this pressing fall of clouds has made a pine
the only place to settle. This makes Crow
with folded wings a black and glistening
pair of hands and his cries, a quick prayer, reach

out through the fog. His eyes get a shimmer
and his ears a song, both like the run off
gurgling at road edge. He sees the stones there
washing strong bodies egg bright, beetle slick.

Daniel David Moses

The One Virtuous Act of the Dictator

The crow sat in the poplar like a black boot.
He was, at first glimpse, a prank,
the remnants of an unruly evening
beside the only rail lines in town.

One of the laces dangled from his beak,
a stick that he had clipped and untied.
When the crow stretched his neck,
he was a boot that reached to the knees.

From the wooden balustrade
he cast his decoration,
it hurried through the branches
in the slapping of its own applause.

When I caught the stick, the crow
quit the tower, his body an adamant march
beyond these houses, back to his bunker
having simply made the trains run on time.

Adam Dickinson

The Lost Hawk

They threw a blanket
over the lost hawk
sitting like an ornament of the age
on the car's high chrome
disoriented by downtown
he'd been hunting ledge pigeons
percolating among
the public buildings, midst the uptown things
the gargoyles, the friezes, the low stone lions
of inner city postal service

these living feathers
quiver to be caught, quiver
like ancient quill-penned poets
tensed to the pause of their breathing ink
touched wet to the blot-point of it, emboldened and
predatory as the black eye
of a terrified bird
bringing its beautiful swift-winged hunger
to the page, to this slab-coloured wilderness
and the falsity and confusion of artificial nightfall
hooded by comfort like a kitchen parrot

what and where
does he believe himself to be
bronzing as he is
into a difficulty, the lackluster
ambergris of this smothering two-handed darkness

the same we use to tuck
our children in
to stop the fear of dreaming with

John B. Lee

Bell Curve

We're learning how to divide the gulls. Pinkness of leg,
thickness of beak, herring or ring-billed. The naked eye
can't tell from a distance. True things, even the matter
-of-factness of a seabird cry, have a tendency

to fly. Fine lines, first V-shaped, then imperceptible
on the horizon. We may slow down, domesticate,
adjust our binoculars, memorize the guidebooks,
move out to the coast, and still not stop novelty: white

-eyed, black-beaked, yellow-footed, brown-hooded, glaucous-winged,
swallow-tailed. We're all taking this course, and we'll all get
some credit. See, it's the common that dictates the wild
undercurrents of interior, surface, or sea.

Madhur Anand

I Saw Your Mate Up the River

I saw your mate up the river
her red crown like pine needles in the snow
soft gray body, a suggestion

You are downstream
with geese that pepper the frozen riverbank
standing slim-legged on the ice
burying their bills in their wings,
their tracks point backward—
arrows in retreat
tracing unworn paths in the snow

You are white-breasted
black-crowned, beak
a curved upholsterer's needle

The geese have been crossing
the path of commuters—
who stop on their afternoon rush home
to mates and frozen riverbanks
gingerly circumvent the geese
laying a new path

For a moment trespassing
the paths they are meant to follow,
watching feather-pressed breasts pass safely.

Anna Bowen

Goose, Plummeting

Look
and you might see the farmer,
his pails set down, gazing up
at the arrowhead flight-pattern of geese—
the precision-point leader heading
two lines in his wake.

The farmer rubs his sore muscles,
tight from the pull of pails, and marvels
at the grace of wings, communal flight.
His shoulders drop as he watches the perfect point
glide through the sky.
He thinks the word *wedge*.

A random shot
rips the silence,
then he witnesses the spiralling down—

one goose plummeting from its place
like ripped tar paper,
a ragged Valkyrie
descending
before the bird smacks the stubbled field.

A second goose pulls
from formation, spears
down to the mark.

Now the taste of storm is in the air.

It leads the farmer to the field
with a crate, water, his wife's wool blanket
for the grounded goose.

Her mate tenderly strokes
her splayed wing
with his beak.

The farmer cradles the wounded goose
in a sling of blanket
and carries her to the barn.
He looks back to nod at her partner,
who follows at a distance, blinking his bead eyes.

In a depression of hay,
her life-mate leans his curved neck onto her breast.
It will be only a day
until the she-goose expires.

After a night of nuzzling her dead body,
the goose flies away at dawn
to catch the draft of another V.

But years later the farmer still tells his wife:

"Every November
I swear that goose
pecks for a moment
at my barn window."

Kate Marshall Flaherty

Swifts

in circles
the day's end gossip
chirped curtly
above their old chimney

theatrical:
melodramatic dives
diverted left or right
at the cathartic edge
then taking again
the twilight of upstage

the play's the thing.
why go home directly
when you can make a scene,
extend an act,
happily prolong
the whole free-flying production?

there's no business like show
and tell and zip and swoop
and chatter together
on a sunset-set
before an audience
stilled by adoration

then it's done;
night drops the final curtain
and the houselights
flicker on in the firmament
to guide the flightless
watchers to their own
less elevated home.

Greg Kennedy

Syrinx

The birds were triggered at dawn. They
sang to Leonardo until he freed them. They

banded Audubon to see if he'd return.
They wrote to John Clare on their eggs:

postage due. They spoke Greek to Virginia,
told Rosa Luxemburg of revolutionary

clouds. The crows made a tiny paper
Joseph Cornell and put him in a box.

The ravens say You lookin' at me? I don't
see anyone else here. The finches want

to see some credentials. The sparrows
insist on their standards; they are not

speaking to the starlings. The pigeons
found it hard to tell the truth

to Flannery O'Connor and hard to tell lies
about Frank McCourt. The albatross

was in on that necktie party from the start.
Birds don't believe in big government or

omertà. We showed them the video,
and when they saw that deer

swallow a chickadee, they were
as shocked as anyone.

Tanis MacDonald

Birds' Songs

My ancestors once told me
there is a Life Tree in the East
where birds ceaselessly sing.

I've long forgotten it
or lost faith in it.
Sitting beside my screen,
to forge a bird's song,
a button is what I click.
Yet the humming from this magic
fails to bring the story back.

This morning, into Bulls Point Loop
where Lake Ontario is near
and Six Nations' people once looked out,
I pause at birds' signs and tiny feeders.
Colorful and beautiful in still poses,
each teaches me a name: American Goldfinch,
Rose-breasted Grosbeak, Blue Jay, Cardinal,
Scarlet Tanager, Red-tailed Thrush,
and Yellow Warbler…

"Morning, little birds"
I call out,
my eyes searching into the deep.
Among lush leaves,
I cannot trace their flight.
But I hear
song after song,
full of joy,
full of freedom,
burst from them,
burst from myself.

"Morning, little birds"...
a whole world of wonders
we sing to each other.

Anna Yin

In the space of ten minutes

two small woodpeckers trying so hard not to fall off
the rough limbs of the lilac that their taps
are ineffectual, beaks bouncing off the branch

a speckled mini-robin transfixed on a patio stone
gazing at itself in a puddle

a baby grackle teetering on the birdbath edge
so long that its mother flies down
slaps him off with her wing

a thin sparrow open-mouthed on the fence
parent placing a shiny black seed in the gape

A crazy surge of love for these baffled
and befuddled creatures …
I must have come outside

the moment after a host of mothers
ejected their young from the nest
perhaps a day or two too soon.

Marilyn Gear Pilling

Kingfisher: Grand River

castanet call
like snapped bones

stiletto beak
stabbing air

crazed headdress
like a maimed fin

whirr of light-
stippled wings

fringed shawl
of blue flame

flash of
rusted belt

tail unfurled
to a torrid fan

furious dance
at sundown

low over
oiled water

the river's
libertine face

bloated then
skewed by

stone dikes
& rutted dams

of black rebar
& shotcrete

Daniel MacIsaac

Elegy for Al Purdy

the blue heron
stands alone
on one leg
knee deep in the black bay at Cootes Paradise
his solitude and studied stillness
like wind-and-water-weathered wood
the broken barkless bone-brittle elm
that sank itself
all but for this
the last and lonely
leafless and unliving branch
thrust up and lighter
for the visible half-movement
when the hard-to-believe-in grey-eyed thing
he is becomes a bird
as it turns the lean curve of its carved head
to show an underwater will
from step-weight on a nearby stone
and then
he spans his wings
and shatters off this boggy shadow glade
like stain on startled glass
and he's buoyant in the blue
and big
enough to carry twice the darkness
by his leaving
these little stolen day-lost
silhouettes of drifting night dropped down
and grown ever-larger farther as they are
until he lands again
outside the lead-sketched light
and in wordless height of draft
becomes the thought of *loft*

and what it is to be
both object and metaphor
all mournful
and uncapturable as wind.

John B. Lee

Triptych for One Loon

I.
Loon on lapping Lake Ontario,
past the salt docks and raked sand.

Suddenly there, the bird
has bobbed up further
from where it plunged—further
than imagined breath could be held.

Alone under the mid-day moon.

II.
Loon stays under so long
you almost forget he descended at all.
You turn back to your book on the beach

and then, like nostalgia, he comes
far from where you expected
he could go.

III.
Loon tilts his straight beak
and tucks his webbed feet for take-off—
flaps rhythmic wings that slap
down and up—loon and his wavy mirror-twin
leaving
a lean V trail.

Disturbed water.

Reading, interrupted.

Kate Marshall Flaherty

What Suffers Into Shadow at the Edges

Listening to the high
loud carpentry of birds
building their bug holes
hammering home
an appetite in the altitude
I am reminded
of a busy and beautiful silence
I have not heard for weeks
oh what lovely rattapallax
above the shingles
of these shelters
with their chimney smokes
dragged grey
with light after rain

everything this April almost Easter
rises wild brown
and heaven fits the sky
while the lonely woodpecker
frames his natural cross
from pileated pine
in this water-flattered gloom
what suffers into shadow at the edges
might suffice

John B. Lee

American Woodcock

Intruder among daffodils, tulips,
cryptic in the mean
neighbour's garden, you sat

planted as a dare with your narrow
bill of pale brown tipped
like a dipping bird into a glass beaker

without the force for swinging back.
We wanted to jab you with our sticks,
make you twitch—*bird puppet*!—

avoid your poker beak;
cage you in a mist net. You just
sat there, caught in our own trap

of indecision, until your short wings
flipped air into flight—
leaving us wild for your name.

Catherine Graham

The Meaning of Starlings

Last night, just as daylight migrated west,
a congregation of starlings a quarter of an hour long
flew eastward past the window.
    It felt like a dismantling of the natural order,
so many birds leaving.
                                        The constant shifting
& winking of individuals in the long flock
tricked the eye into seeing counterfeit letters.
    A message, perhaps? Save our ship?

We are used to dragging our human business
across a stupefied & uncomprehending Nature.
    Deer jump through picture windows
& crash around livingrooms in shock.
    Pheasants explode from roadside ditches
into the windshields of passing cars. Sometimes
a bird will fly at a window over & over
    & die trying to enter the reflected sky.
Once, after bringing in the laundry,
    my neighbour released a hummingbird
from a floral towel. Its confusion seemed
somehow endearing to her.

        We cannot expect them
to understand our highly evolved complexities.
But, as the final spoonful of daylight
evaporated among the bare arms of a distant elm
    and the last few birds flew past
        forming letters in a language
I couldn't read, my own puzzled reflection
gradually replaced a multitude of starlings
        in a darkened windowpane.

Bernadette Rule

WILD CREATURES

"Urban people consider it strange that deer are living in such numbers in our neighbourhoods. But then, why is it such a surprise? What made us assume that a city would be a place where the only neighbours would be other people?"
—**Daniel Coleman**, *Yardwork*[36]

[36] Daniel Coleman, *Yardwork: A Biography of an Urban Place* (James Street North Books, 2017), p. 177.

Invisible Deer

"Daddy, take us to see the invisible deer," my children said.

"But I already have," I said. "Can't you see? They are all around us."

"Stop joking," they said. "Take us really."

"But it was only yesterday that we saw the glass deer, and the day before that, the ice deer, and before that, the atomic deer, and last week, we went to see the memory deer and the deer that smoulder in the grass."

"We know, Daddy, but we are so bored and the invisible deer are special."

"Okay, my little pink deer with antlers that are pigtails. I'll take you."

We got in the car and drove behind the shopping mall. We parked at the very end of the parking lot, near a small thicket of trees. I waited a moment to turn the car off while we listened to the end of our favourite song. Then we all climbed out.

"Ready?" I said.

"Ready," they said.

And we closed the four car doors together. We'd practiced this and we could do it with precision. There was a single sound as if we were closing one very large family-sized car door.

"Now let's look for deer," I said.

Walking into the thicket was like walking into a building. It was cooler as if, like the mall, it was air conditioned, but it was a different, thicker air. It was darker, too. There was a kind of emptiness, a hush. Only the shadows and whispers of birds, the leaf-stirring sounds of squirrels and other small animals.

"Do you see them?" I whispered.

"Where, Daddy?" my children asked. I pointed high into the branches of some trees beyond a small clearing.

"Daddy," my youngest said. "You're silly. Deer can't fly. They can't climb. They don't own invisible ladders."

"I have an invisible ladder," I said. "Sometimes I climb into the clouds."

"Why do you do that, Daddy?"

"So I can run my hands through the cloud material. So I can know what it will be like to be old," I said.

Gary Barwin

Looking for a Fast Buck

For four years and four months
I took the road through the woods
twice a day and more
and only saw the deer six times.
I still believe they were there
at least six hundred times,
but I wasn't quick or lucky
enough to spot them.

Sometimes
I looked so hard each branch
became a rack. Whole hillsides
of deer raised their heads
with the wind and spent
some cool contempt on me
before fleeing on all sides,
leaving me only mundane meadows.

Bernadette Rule

Sunrise over the Grand River

the pink sky yawns above my morning commute
white clouds lengthen across the horizon
the sun floats
my car dips toward the river valley
mist hovers around thickets of maple, stout conifers
grassy mounds and leafy shrubs pad the banks
crossing the bridge, a glance at the dark moving water

on the rise, the road widens
three lanes of highway curl east, two west
a narrow patch of greenery at the junction
approaching my exit
          two deer   dash out
red flare   the car in front   brakes
          brown fur   hurtling across
fender and hind legs   collide   crack
the youngling   tumbles and spins   into the ditch

I brake in staccato jerks
the car spasms left, right in the lane
tea sloshes, purse slides
migrating traffic vacillates a moment
then rolls on like the river

Paula Kienapple-Summers

Disappointment in the Masonry

There is little doubt
that bats are in the chimney.
At dusk, you can hear
the folded sheets
of their slender ascent,
a private appearance
over rooftops,
the steam from a bath
that has just been filled.

Their modesty confounds us.
They dart in the cover of tree tops
as though rushing from bathrooms to dress.
When we see them in the dark
we are half of the mind
they are leaves we've mistaken.

One evening, something
clung to the ceiling
above the fireplace,
cramped in its brown shiver,
the body of an old man
hunched before a tub.
We didn't think to get
the paddle or the broom,
but opened all of the windows,
turned out the lamps,
and felt for the railing to the street,
its cold abashment
working blindly in our hands.

Adam Dickinson

To God, as a Small Pest

The squirrel scrambling, light-as-air, over the roof
is you, is it not? The roaming slope
to peak, across and down, scritches
delicate as destruction,
                                        shows that old animal
spirit trying to find a way in, never yet
poking a grey head past the edge of the skylight,
so I may see.

                              I believe, now,
you have no pride: an imagination
that ranges wildly, seizing any
shape that fits, adopting
what'll do,
                         with a relentless playfulness,
and your insidious intent;
                                             and I resist
this recognition, as strongly
as the gnawing at my fascia, soffit,
that I imagine comes next, and tense and listen for.

     I rather looked for you in the birds gathered
about the feeder, the many separate
thoughts one has, the argue and agreement
of wings, and a hungry abandon to the truth
of contending against another winter's advent.

New this Fall is the balled nest of leaves no bird
comes near, that the highest-reaching branches of the ash
lift eye level to the attic room I hole in.
You're home. Comfort and warning
co-habit,

as when I stood below, preparing
breakfast, and happened to look, you
halfway up the trunk, our eyes locked
and I wondered what,
what was that small round
black thing
you held in your mouth?

John Terpstra

Barnesdale Blvd, Ohròn:wakon[37]

Two pillars at the corner of Main Street
monuments now missing their iron bars
once meant to separate the public from the private
this place used to be a haven for the wealthy
doctors and lawyers and conmen
bell boys running to and from homes
carrying news from the outside world
I am a (trans)plant to Barnesdale Blvd
an imperfect match
one of many from a failing species, *tenants*
dreaming of home ownership, a group now severed
from genealogies rooted in the Blvd's originators
the suburban is merely a façade
I learn from the traces of extra human life
who greet me every day without malice
a young raccoon is perched on the rooftop to my right,
as I stand on the deck with tea in hand
co-existing, the wind rummaging through our furs
there's a tawny rabbit to my left
I look down from my deck as it snips away at daylilies
she is unbothered by my gaze, *I think*
her earth tones complement a field of fallen magnolia petals
magnolia coincides with maple who shades me
no talk of money, no whispers of job promotions
only music, the bustling of leaves, a sound predating
horse carriages and black gates and the human
a timeless symphony persists *despite* the suburban
I sip chamomile and watch the squirrels traverse a network
of greens, pinks, yellows, uninhibited by polite society.

Linzey Corridon

---

37 *Ohròn:wakon* is the Kanienkeha (Mohawk) name for Hamilton, and means "In the ditch, or ravine."

Home in the Fall

And there they were, a troupe
Of boys on the edge
Of their limestone stage.
Sliced wedge of earth
Fashioned by a nameless creek
and some unhuman age.

Water. Stone. Light.
pulsing Blood
in flight.

The ruddy faced boys,
Innocents, tread over leaves
Golden, decaying, scattered;
Carefully picking
their upstream way among
rocks strewn, shattered.

And in their hands, the players
Flash crude spears and bows
Of imagined Iroquois make.
They gambol forward,
This company of emigres,
On the bottom of the glacial lake.

Fire. Fear. Fight.
pulsing Blood
In flight.

I was born here.
Niagara in the Fall is home
I return for holidays.
We wind along the creek bottom.

Tracing the faint ways
Of our other selves who
Moved, shapeless shades
Shifting in the dappled light
Among the greys and graves
Of shaking shale
Scrabbled hard amidst
White pine and Shagbark
And the burrowing Seven-Mile creek
Chuckling softly as it shears
The world apart.

And there they are, a school
of salmon, vermicular and torsional,
Muscles humped above the flow
Strained and stupefied
Against the mundane force
Of gravity, and
Of *libido dominandi*.

The boys' howls echo still
Off the rock and water,
through the light.
And the churn of flesh,
And the crack of sticks,
Bear witness to approaching night.

This ancient blood now sees the sun:
What had we done?
In the full noon of pastoral day:
What part had we been called to play?

And as we, careless, unclenched our hand
We grasped and grasped
Our native land.

Doug Sikkema

A Philosophy of Zoos

Monotheism drove them from the ancient
temple, replaced the horse goddess Epona,
the golden calf, the jaguar, the veneration

of every large and potent animal species
with the worship of an abstract god. Animal
demoted to demon.

How, then, to experience the holy shiver?
How to look into the eyes
of powerful alien beings
and experience the fear and awe
we once found there?

Linda Frank

INSECTS

"The Devil's darning needle, ear sewer, eye poker, ear cutter, eye snatcher. Horse stinger. Troll's spindle."
—**Linda Frank**, "Dragonfly"[38]

[38] From Linda Frank, *Divided* (James Street North Books, 2018), p. 6.

Divided

Insect from Latin *insectum* (animal) means *divided* (animal) or *cut into sections*

He tells me how much he hates them.
He shivers when he flicks on the light
and cockroaches tear across
his floor. Squirms when silverfish
scuttle round the drain of his tub.

Insects fly at you, he says. They crawl up your legs
buzz at the screen. They bite. Feed
on your blood. If he could bring himself
to touch them, he'd lash out
and crush them.

I know they're strange creatures. They breathe
without lungs. Their blood flows freely
through their body cavity, no veins
or arteries. No ears. Eyes
on either side of their head. They see
mosaic images
wear their skeletons on the outside.

How alien they are to him, yet how deeply present
to me. And how divided we are
about their place in our world.

Linda Frank

Ko, Revolution

My first miracle was the monarch butterfly; the way she looked around
Miss Mitten's grade two classroom, climbed her twig in the aquarium,
arced her slow, wet wings, charged them with flight. More

marvellous than Clark Kent squeezing into the telephone booth
on Melville Street in Dundas, morphing into Superman. And what, by
the way,
did he do with his shoes, his suit, his black-rimmed glasses?

Chung Fu, Inner Truth

We were paddling down the Grand, we were pulling in at night.
The river spoke in firefly. Phrases lit like filament, flung like seed. Stars
above, stars in the prickling grass. A milky way. I dreamed a democracy

where flowering meadows commanded political will. Plants
were invited to speak their minds and hedge-fund managers tuned
their ears to grasshoppers, horseflies, the whiney No-See-Ums.

Cornelia Hoogland

Dragonfly

i

seraph wings
softly shimmering

luminous prisms
caught in gossamer

celestial messenger
skimming

at lightspeed over
still water

ii

guardian hovers
& churns

a gyring tumult
& catapults

transfigured
turbocharged

gunship rotors
scourging thin air

Daniel MacIsaac

Dragonfly

The Devil's darning needle, ear sewer, eye poker, ear cutter,
eye snatcher. Horse stinger. Troll's spindle.
The adder's servant, it follows
snakes around and stitches them up when they are injured.

August god, lady of the weeping willow, widow skimmer,
water witch. The Devil's little horse sent by Satan
to create chaos
to steal people's souls.

Linda Frank

God's Bits of Wood

She is not the long birch pole Deda carved,
not a ticking wheel for measuring steps—

not a "tool thing" at all.
walking stick—

she's a living stem of a bug,
a sapling insect,

her hopping busy bark,
match-thin

she genuflects,
rubs her twig hands together

as if before a feast
or sacred ablution—

No wings, nor honeycomb eyes,
no beetle gloss nor stinger

This bug is bipedal—she, like me, just
wood wisps in the huge forest—

Kate Marshall Flaherty

Orb Weaver

Surrounded, detached, in measureless oceans of space,
Ceaselessly musing, venturing, throwing, seeking the spheres to connect them,
Till the bridge you will need be form'd, till the ductile anchor hold,
Till the gossamer thread you fling catch somewhere, O my soul.
—Walt Whitman, "A Noiseless Patient Spider"

Ceaselessly musing, venturing, throwing, seeking the spheres to
connect them
The diaphanous filament you float on the wind
Till the gossamer thread you fling catch somewhere, O my soul
The dragline and the drop line

The diaphanous filament you float on the wind
Your slow folding and unfolding of legs
The dragline and the drop line
My presence of no concern to you

Your slow folding and unfolding of legs
You weave between the branches of the cedar
My presence of no concern to you
You weave, and the sunlight shines the threads silver

You weave between the branches of the cedar
Till the bridge you will need be form'd, till the ductile anchor hold
You weave, and the sunlight shines the threads silver
Surrounded, detached, in measureless oceans of space

Linda Frank

Pool Fly

Both feet in chlorinated droplets,
forehead bright as grassblades backlit
by sun, you stand still
on my knuckle.

I run my fingernail
beneath a wing stuck to itself.
I slide the other between
pinched fingers and
        you let me.

Vibration. Soft and sharp. Movement
without takeoff. I lift you to my eyes
and (I swear) you face me,
leaning forward as

those back legs, quick and sure,
glide up and down—level your wings
in their veined translucence,
        refract light.

Thank you. For the invitation to a long look

though all six legs
worked fine.

Elise Arsenault

Buzz

It's not just me, there's also you,
Both of us up and unable
To take a break, you from buzzing

That ten-watt bulb, me from being
Awake. Why do I think the two
Situations are linked? What do

I care? The thought that a fly might
Be stuck in some facsimile
Of a tragic plot, *Electron*

and Nucleus, the twain never
To meet, ought not to bore me. Love,
Even one so meagre, deserves,

I was taught, a consummation.
But what your motive toward the light
Gets from me is irritation.

If you tick against that glass once
More, I'm afraid it might push me
Through one of the many new cracks

In my old composure. Oh, tick
Again and the live wiring of
My brain will short out, electrons

Doing their bit for comedy,
A sputtered climax, which would, yes,
Improve on this dead end we're in.

I lay me down, praying you will
Tick once more, even while the buzz
Of reason reminds me none of

My prayers have been answered before.
To calm me more it questions why
I don't try that switch by the door.

I don't know any more. I don't
Know. Even with my body so
Far away, it should be easy

As breaking glass. A forefinger
And thumb made out of the darkness
Pinching us out of existence—

Daniel David Moses

Apoid Wasps

The invisible is what makes visible. The structure
of the visible which does not itself appear.
—Maurice Merleau-Ponty

There is a natal nest.

Hollow stems, leaf straws,
naturally-formed roundhouse.

The apoid wasps make a tubular home for their *natal.*

Or: they take one—

Formerly occupied homes
of carpenter bees and other insects[39]—

whose larval dependents
are hiding in their homemade houses,

or had already left the premises
when the wasps came and took it.

Temporarily or permanent vacation, it's unclear.

On occasions the Hurons and Algonquins would journey to the south
to war with tribes south of Lake Ontario. These tribes, the Mohawks,
Senecas, Oneidas, Onondagas, Cayugas and later the Tuscaroras, joined
together to form the Six Nations Confederacy for protection from the
roving Hurons.

---

39 Kyla Ercit, "Size and sex of cricket prey predict capture by sphecid wasp," in *Ecological Entomology* 39:2 (2013), 195-202. [Author's note.]

And then they hunt.

The families Sphecidae and Crabronidae hunt
and provision arthropods for their offspring

Massacred crickets
dragged home like a crumpled umbrella,
little larval lunch.

Locating the domicile
and rigging its threshold to count
the ins and outs crucial to verification
of the habits of a true predator.[40] *Xantholinus elegans*

A recent accidental introduction to North America as it was not included in Smetana (1990) and the earliest specimen known is from 2007, native range is distributed widely in the western Palearctic region and recorded from Austria, Belgium, Bosnia, Herzegovina, Czech Republic, France, Great Britain, Germany, Hungary, Ireland, Italy, Luxembourg, The Netherlands, Poland, Slovakia and Spain.

By definition a killer will not let you watch the kill.

You have to use the stand-in,

the dummy for death-making, the analogue of evidence.

Indirectly plotted data points from *random positions*
within our plot at each site: grainy photos from the very mouth
of the situation.

---

40 Adam J. Brunke and C.G. Majka, "The Adventive genus Xantholinus Dejean in North America: new records and a synthesis of distributional data," *ZooKeys* 65 (2010), 51-61. [Author's note.]

With the highest proportion of correctly sorted observations
determined by jackknifing the data you can produce.

A reasonable model of a standard death.

The model stands in for the *thing itself*—

an effective technique for the past, a less reliable predictor

of orthogonal capture, of arthropods; their prospects
for staying alive in the vicinity of a temporary
degree of freedom (df) = 1.

Worse odds for females.

Always dip-zagging,
and clinging thickly
because of *conspicuous eggs*;

suffer higher predation for having been built to carry.

The hunters return, carrying the hunted, they cross
the trip-line of their found or stolen homes:

the science counter clicks exactly once.

In July 1748 the Six Nations defeated their enemies the Hurons and went on to defeat the Neutrals. After this defeat the Grand River became the hunting grounds of the Six Nations or Iroquois, with no major tribe living there.

How many more curled-up inside learning how to wait it out?

Karen Houle

Rusty Patch Bumblebee

I am beginning to know you,
Phlox gymnasts, your tiny arms working the swaying flower heads
A spray of silken purple flowers
each one the intimacy of suckling
your instinct like perpetual infanthood
instead of swallowing, you are the tongue
that carries nectar to the throat

You are the intricacy of lovemaking
How did you get awarded the most sensual job?
To carry the perpetuity of reproduction against your thigh
like an afterthought.

Anna Bowen

Father Demetrius's Bees

All day over the canola,
small prayers for the sun.
If love could quit its veins, its chemical language,
the airy transmogrification of trembling hands,
the clots that build dark hills in the chest,
it would be these small sparks, these lanterns
that explain plants to each other,
that return home at night,
and write the first desires of things
in moonlit sugar.

Because we cannot simply stand in the sun,
because there is no single honeysuckle,
no hummingbird tuning the valves of the heart,
they work in the name of abundance.
To live is to stick to things, honey in the hands,
the simplest wish crowded with wings.

It is said that when the beekeeper retires,
he becomes allergic to the venom of bees.
What love asks so much?
All day over the canola,
the fresh wax of introductions,
the first deposits of fat
in the catacombs of the heart.

Adam Dickinson

Home

This GMO-caused toxin (that now pervades pollen)
contains something that disorients the bees so that they can't
find their way back to their hives.
—letter from a friend

We carried water from the well to the fields
for our neighbours—harvest time on our uncle's farm.
Roast chicken and five kinds of pie at noon dinner.
Mid-afternoon lemonade in sweet clover, bees
at the hum. Straw in golden drifts
in the fields.
Later, night air on our burnt faces,
windows rolled down, the short drive home
to our farm. A huge, sated moon.
The crickets' calling song, sobsong of frogs.
Rivery smell of the Maitland.

A world
that disappeared
in tandem with our childhood.

Half a lifetime later, driving to work in snarled
city traffic, the radio tuned to classical CBC—
Va, pensiero, sull'ali dorate ...
a melody so infused with longing that I, who rarely
cry, suddenly could not see
the road. I did not then know that it was
Verdi's *Chorus of the Hebrew Slaves*—exiles
yearning for their homeland.

Did not then know
about the bees.

Marilyn Gear Pilling

FLOWERS AND PLANTS

"Etymologically, 'anthology' refers to a collection of flowers, varied species of blooms selected and arranged so that they look like they belong together. Since the term's modern origins in the seventeenth century, multiplicity has always been the form's selling point: the provision in one volume of very different voices and concerns that nonetheless have some kind of collective force."

—**Clare Bucknell**, "What Do We Want from Poetry in Times of Crisis?"[41]

[41] Clare Bucknell, "What Do We Want from Poetry in Times of Crisis?" *New Yorker* Dec 22, 2020.

Queen Anne's Lace

Our hosts had thought of everything—
Queen Anne's lace and chicory
to line the lonely roads north in profusion,
like welcomers along a procession route,
cheering us, waving us on (delftware,
blue and white, in ditches and dry fields)
to where the road ends and the land.

There's more than enough, they say,
the comfort, grace, and excess
of hospitality—food and drink and warmth
and love and life. The lights of cottages
across the lake go out one by one, and we rest safe,
as raccoons, bears—all creatures of the night—
creep out of caves to do their rounds.

Sheryl Loeffler

Will It?

Just as the right verb for yellow hits the throat, petals
dry up and green leaves emerge. This is March's grammar.
Inversions begging questions. *Forsythia* escapes

English hedgerows to write down rules in Mandarin script.
Communication is a bringing in. Rearrange
cut branches while there's hope for ornament or prayer.

Expand the vocabulary of interiors.
Enlighten the gardener's kitchen, her cloudy head.

Madhur Anand

Escarpment

Trout lily.

Fins of teeth slitting the earth,
writhing with worms.

Jack-in-the-pulpit.

The man inside the hooded leaf
holding his voice for the gust.

O

how red petals come brutal
through the white trilliums of Niagara.

Catherine Graham

Reclamation

I don't own my lungs,
I inherited them.
Grief fused,
Carcinoma.
Diaphragm stretches with the tide of abandon and attack,
Like some clumsy and desperate thing struggling to survive.

Shallow inhale,
Restrained exhale.

The rhythm of grief.
This is my body,
Pavement poured over the sediments of my ancestors' bones.
Hostage soil,
Tarred over wild and savage earth.

Every moment I am alive,
I am growing medicine inside me.

Hawthorne, Yarrow, Nettle, Motherwort, allies of my body.
Blooming through pavement like a chronicle of resistance,
A reminder of what stood here before, and what continues to grow
despite being called weeds.

Despite being burned, being called useless, being relocated and forced
into lands where they thought I wouldn't survive.

This is my reclamation of self.

I am growing medicine for the generations that will inherit me.

Alyssa General

Dandelion

Let's face it—I'm envious.
Your ubiquity. Your tenacity.
You're everywhere. You're rooted.

I'm nowhere. A nomad. But
you're a traveller, too, you say.
You and your kin put down roots

wherever I try to make my home.
Vagrant, trespasser, squatter—you've
made me into a sapper, a poisoner.

You think to make a case for your benignity.
The healing milk of your veins. The rich
green of your leaves for salads, wine.

Birds and bees and children love
your seeds, your nectar, your bright beauty.
Yellow spots of pollen on each other's chins—

butter, we called them—and picked bouquets
for our mothers, who put them in water
in plastic glasses for the afternoon table.

Your solitary white head rises above
a wet mat of brown leaves and grass
as I turn off the November highway—Why aren't you

dead yet? Everything else is!—
seeds poised to parachute into next year.
I can't deny your virtuosity.

I can't deny your attraction.
I can't deny my bitter love.
And I can't get rid of you.

Sheryl Loeffler

Dandelions at Dusk

Struck by the tilting light,
the dandelions flare,
a fire in a match-
stick forest. So stop. Watch

it burn. Even that tame
a patch of flame teaches
something. Maybe that night
won't quite put the embers

out. Or maybe you learn
to forget. The field
flares up in stars. Daylight.
Do you remember it?

Daniel David Moses

September: Hay fever, Hogwash, and Goldenrod

Calumny!
Goldenrod is not ragweed;
it doesn't make you sneeze,
it doesn't kick you in the sinuses

Victim of vicious smear campaigns,
goldenrod is simply late summer sunshine
incarnate, innocent, splendid
green-handled torches
lighting the way for wing-weary
bees dim-eyed from long days' work.
If you are allergic to beauty,
you have a problem
beyond the range of antihistamines.

So don't project your prickly grief
over the shutting down of August
onto the burnished gold
of sunset fields aging into autumn.
Don't blame or shame
but sit a moment in September
by a roadside or a meadow
and get to know your dark blonde neighbour,
so magnificent and so maligned.

Greg Kennedy

October Cornfield

Tarnished gold
burnished old age of the crop
doesn't diminish
the cobless pizzazz
of the stalk-whispered vespers,
the open air aves,
the husk-hungry jazz
of the breeze as it passes
and sashays so sassily
just out of sight.
God and I listen
and dance with delight
to that old razzle dazzle
of wind-wrestled tassles.
Irascible stalks form
a saw-toothed wind castle
and God's in his chasuble
(me, I've come casual)
to witness this sensuous
soughing chanson,
the warp and woof weaving
of wind in the stalks.

So glad my ears were picked.

Bernadette Rule

The Corn

I'd already lost my hair. Now my sun-
fed children have been taken somewhere. Next

I'll lose those comfortable shoes of mud
to the cold, will be unconcerned. I no

longer need a firm foothold after all.
There's no flood of light anymore—to stand

in, to turn towards. The low sun's a trickle
that lays only shadows out (and they don't

move or fulfill one or feed some). Nor do
they do a thing for one's colour. One's left

with just these growing crystals of frost. No
childish ears to get brightly wet behind,

no hands to hold you as you stand whispering
about the land. No one you could even

wave hello or goodbye. My hands caressed
the emptiness, grew as heavy as ice.

They dropped off; and, soon I'd guess the rest of
me will be ready to follow. Down through

the ice-bound soil to underground fields where
stars are planted in hills. At least that's what

I've seen staring through the frost. Light will not
be lost but will grow and bud green again.

Daniel David Moses

Invasive Species

They are not native,
the Queen Anne's Lace, chicory
and birdsfoot trefoil
that add so much to the country drive,
as they wave back and forth
from the shoulder of the road.

Their success, I have read,
is measured in how well they adapt
to harsh conditions,
how they thrive
in adverse circumstances.

When my parents invaded
from overseas,
spilling like bilge, like zebra mussels,
some would say,
from the hold of a boat,
they lived in a driving shed
attached to a barn.
The farmer, and the farm work,
were brutal. My parents did better
than survive.

The nature guide further states
that non-native trees
may add a green splash to the landscape,
but do not attract insects,
which are adapted to native trees,
and therefore do not interest
or attract birds.

I stand here, a non-native son,
though born on this soil,
and walk my walk,
banging through the woods,
cowbell around my neck,
head in a cloud of bugs,
birds nesting in my beard,
searching for a place that will call me home.

John Terpstra

FARMING AND GARDENING

"There are seeds that lie for decades in the soil, waiting for the right conditions before springing to life. Good work is that which creates the conditions for such life to burst forth from the whole of the creation."

—**Ragan Sutterfield**, *Wendell Berry and the Given Life*[42]

[42] From Ragan Sutterfield, *Wendell Berry and the Given Life* (Franciscan Media, 2017), reprinted by permission of the publisher.

Looming

In the toehold of Palermo,
born Loyalists,
Jerusha Currie married
John Solmon Hager.

The Hager brothers spread
like other invasive species
filling in Bible lines and lots
with flesh writ

John deferred the sacred land of the
ceremony of the white dog
to found Middleport.
There Jerusha birthed fourteen,

wove fabric for their backs
woke them early for chores
fed their meagre hopes with
verses and oats.

In 1853, John Solomon died,
drowned in the wet swamp
of a cough, their eldest,
caught under a felled tree's vengeance

the child within her then,
dead within the same year;
father, son and holy ghost.
The widow wore a path

back and forth from barn
lay hay, pulled swollen udders
rccalling her cow-eyed youth
with a flank pat.

Hob-stoke stooped
sweet sweat smell mixed with
acrid stink of worn bladder and ample girth
of let down and let down.

Her man-sized hands
shifted shuttle, warp and weft
flax fiber and fleece
grandiose homespun.

Elizabeth Tessier

Dear Arne & Marie-Françoise,

you were asking.

   It's about whether to build the ewes' roof shade
with three ventricles, north, south-east & south-west,
thinking of sun & hours.

   It's about whether that boy got all the barbed wire
out of the old fence row before the horses gash themselves.

   It's about the goof who kicked over the red currants
after picking them so carefully.

   It's about red currants.

   It's about hay fever in the mow, the air thick,
your throat so sore
you'd swallow it whole if you could swallow
   but you can't,
about letting the Mennonites surpass you, heaving bale
from wagon to loft, the wagon load getting
lower & lower, the mow higher & higher,
the dust fawn on your jeans, their black pants;
still throwing, "Shall we take a breather?" and
   they mean it,
   puff, puff
and it's back to the throwing, 'refreshment'
a wimpy thing for "die englische Leit"—though you
make it anyway and leave it in a thermos handy
just in case they're kind to themselves.

It's about moving these things around, bales,
'produce', or 'cash crop', cedar posts, a heifer,
topsoil, or manure, or stones, from here to here to here
and back again like a tidal helix, year in
year winking out. About borrowing
or renting trucks or trailers to do this.

It's about selling the second cut because the barn
is busting with surprise over the first,
spilling its gills with bales cured
to a memory of sweetwater green,
and about how much for,
and about ads. It's about reading the Classifieds
with avidity, about really having arrived
here because you
read the Classifieds before the Headlines.

It's about misprints. (Also about busted fan belts,
and white currants.)

It's about shear bolts shearing on the post hole auger
until the old Latvian teaches you to run the tractor on idle
and stall it before shearing another,
about the sizes of stones in stony ground the river's old spillway and
what it must have been like when they opened this land up
without engines, a mere 100 years ago, a wink ago.

About turning up a fossil set in sand, a freshwater shell,
about there being lots of them, keeping you company,
fluting from auricles of clay & rock under your wading feet,
piping you to the barn to feed beasts,
"We were here first and we are still here. Welcome!"

About turning up Latvians in the stony landscape of
modest Ontario esker, trail of the black walnut Mennonites,
black Irish, red Scots; about help, & neighbours,
& the barter system,
keeping you company, making you welcome.

About being well come here. And above all about
black currants, an affair of the heart.

About penny auctions, the neighbours turning out
to scupper the bank by bidding down the bankrupt's
assets, lower & lower,
returning them to him the next day,
pumping him blood,
keeping him on the land, there but for the grace of god.

About the old Ukrainian's wife out west,
his ex-non-wife
who may have changed all our lives here, fighting unto death
in the courts to be awarded half the farm
after 42 years of tending it, their children, & him.

About the local cop who knows how many farm husbands
beat their wives and abuse their children, and who,
and where,
lot & concession;
and about action groups who meet to discuss this
and advertise in the Classifieds.
About rage,
and exhaustion,
and about sanctuary and how tenuous that is,
the more so where everybody knows everybody.

About sanctuary.
About being come here, about choosing this,
about harbouring here, runaground,
about husbanding, conservatrix,
about being covered in lint of animal hair and pheromones
of animal smells and esters of fruit, shelling
till your green thumb hurts, picking
till your nails gush red, feeding
bales, baling feed for the thumping
great, ten-ventricled heart of the circulatory world,
fruits of earth, of labour, of wrath, of love.
About being
here, while we're here.

Here you are—

you're welcome.

Mia Anderson

Beetroot

The ore of her thinking
is red,
like the flush from standing
too quickly
at the end of a day of gardening.
Her fingers are asparagus stalks,
stubbed and coiled cucumbers,
thick from years of having carried the charge
of her burly, grandmotherly care,
the pots of turnip
that needed lugging to the kitchen.
She digs her hands in the soil,
abstracts the weeds
with the informality of a doctor
who has decorated a lifetime
in the service of a single organ.
When she works, the rose of her kerchief
covers her hair.
She wipes her forearm against it to rest,
the dirt has dried in the folds
and falls away crisply
like heels of rye that have been opened
over borscht.

Adam Dickinson

Amherst Island[43]

Refined, terra firma,
this land is home to my state.
I belong to the countryside where
fresh grass and calla lilies lie.

Though the sun makes my skin dry outside,
I try to set aside the fettle of my dermis
for the conditions of the subdivide.
And I love it.

The blood I shed and the tears I cry
go into plucking prickly weeds that show
no mercy, and gnawing on wheat strands,
uprooting grain with my fingertips.

Hard labor's touch puts the sweat on my face
and corset on my sides:
it's hot in the west
and I've got a fast metabolism.

A day's work means losing
weight like wool shed
off a sheared sheep, shaving down
my 90-pound body and perspiring
until the evening's sunset.

---

[43] A Spoken Word poem, in response to the watercolour painting "The Cedars' Farm, Amherst Island" by Daniel Fowler (1810-1894), in the permanent collection of the Art Gallery of Hamilton. A video of Jaidyn Fenton performing her poem was made for the AGH by photographer/videographer Tyler Tekatch: go to the QR code on the Contents page of this anthology.

Summertime got me pickin'
apple trees for breakfast,
n' pluckin' strawberry shrubs for dinner.
Stomach says, abide in organics—
it's the ranch's way of life.
Besides, acidic fruit is better than
eating processed foods,
and fresh pulp is the definition of health.

No finer taste than guava's juices
re-fueling my body with its natural sugars,
rolling across my taste buds
and satisfying my palate.

Cedars' Farm is a planter's dream.
Seedlings from the womb of dirt
turn into precious buds that
become botanical posies.

Marigolds, petunias, lantanas fill
my flower fields just as my horses fill
their wooden stables. Appaloosa, warm-blooded,
Mustang, Akhal-Teke and Dutch,
each horse a taste of bilingual harmony.
All livestock bear their weight
in sustaining marketplace foods,
been carriers of the richest ingredients since 1989.

Mama cows are milked by their udders
bringing mounds of dairy that is molded
into bundles of brie and gouda, friulano or
brise du matin for the locals
and the Butterfields' kids next door to enjoy.

Large eggs are laid by the mother hen.
Nothing but protein sacs solidified
in egg white casings, filled with yolk.
Makes a delightful addition to
blackberry cobbler and crème brûlée.

On the Amherst estate, tractors are corollas.
There ain't no difference between skidders
and the mobile ways of the western world,
using high-speed mechanical engines
and treading through grassy fields
like 80 on a freeway.

I'd rather drive my digger than stride
barefoot on milk thistle, tippy toeing
around wet mud and the occasional "dropping".
Turf tires got nothin' on a tiller's way of walking.
Pulling n' hauling rocks and brush
to clear the path for pastures,
making way for fresh dirt
and new life on the underground.

Makes me smile when I think about it;
sowing seed into loam and
starting from scratch with the help of God,
birthing fresh vegetables from earth to table.
I weep happily when I see a new
bud in the midst of a thousand specks
of soil. It's like watching a newborn spurt
from infancy's subtle stages of stillness.

Suburbanites call it “gestation”,
but us tillers call it fertilization,
germination or the “ground’s maternity,”
leaving endless fields of cornrows,
and plump peppers plucked from new vines.

Reminds me of my family,
embracing country living back home.
Mom and dad would be tending to the breadfruit trees,
pouring mulch and pruning dead branches,

while I’d be collecting my favourite fruit
in woven baskets: sweet pomegranate,
and spreading lavender oil around each crop
to keep the rabbits away.

You could grow the most beautiful things
with the smallest heap of soil because
it was so abundant in vitamins and minerals.
The sun would just smile at each crop and
they would flourish into six-foot-tall figures.

Jamaica.
3000 miles away from me
and I
on the Amherst.

Jaidyn Fenton

The Orchard Song

The farmer's son
Climbs up among
The branches of the night.
He's always dreamed
Of harvesting
A moon so sweet, so ripe.

His eyes are full of silver
--He's always had far sight
Beyond his father's land
He sees
A city made of light.

How many moons
Will be enough
For him to leave the farm?
All the taxes
The land carries,
The old man's broken bones.

The old man's eyes are water,
That second kind of sight.
Beneath the tree of night
He met
A woman made of clay.

The farmer's wife
Will lose her son
—He'll tarnish in the town.
He'll spend himself,
He'll lose his way,
Counterfeiting the moon.

The woman's eyes are oceans
　　　—She's always seen her boy
Climb up the tree of day,
　　　At play
—The apple of her eye.

Daniel David Moses

Hibiscus

Haematoma: and the blood
  will out—from in you damaged, from in the sheep's
    ear swiped by the dog, wherever

the injured blood pools
  and then outs in due course:
    the telltale river of oath between us

shepherd and sheepfold folded into this river-basin
  like a swipe,
    bonded as flesh.

Sex is trauma, technically—
  yet the body's best guest
    save the soul (if soul is

guest, not host: if host
  and guest are different.
    They may not be.)

All your loves are linked:
  the mole runs underground the colour
    of a bruise.

Kingfisher's back, and the next get of lambs
  queues up for Tuesday, the first round jamming the gates
    of their creep, rotund.

The little dog lies at the river's edge.
  The moon is old.
    The big dog barks from the yard,

his big mitts that paff sheep,
    socko,
        padding the mud.

Trauma of the spirit
    where spirit's different (it may not be)
        speaks too in blood, in wearing out.

Letting blood
    is an old cure.
        Birth is trauma too.

The sheep manage,
    but the shepherd helps.
        Between us we manage.

'Feed my lambs': the imperative
    poises like an alarm clock,
        it goes off, and off. There is no escape.

You may be wounded.
    There is no escape.
        Tomorrow the tree-swallows, later the brown thrasher.

George MacDonald writes a kids' story of
    a lost sheep and a lost son,
        a Gaelic rewrite of the prodigal.

How we hurt to
    save our lambs.
        But also we hurt.

Are we at home here?
  Do we know it?
    That's everything, that's all there is:

at home, and knowing it.
  Wounded with love of it knowing it.
    Break-hearted with birth into

this river basin like a letting.
  The river licks by,
    licking the old weeds.

One March a borealis bred
  such a giant
    stain of red in the sky

above the barn you'd've said an afterbirth
  bloomed there like a hibiscus, you'd've said
    the world's bearing its trauma, birthing itself,

budding open, oh!
  (And a lamb and a little girl
    were born that night, both named Sarah.)

I'm lashed to this life like a birthing,
  tangled in bonds of flesh
    and there's no out.

Off, and off, it goes
  and I'm swinged to the quick
    and loving. And there is no help for it.

The barn-swallows
    have breasts the colour of the borealis
        and the Sarahs grow and grow.

The little dog
    rests at my feet
        at the river's edge.

Mia Anderson

The Barn

Through the gaps in her teeth
we see out of her smile,
we various Jonahs
each in a private state of flight
unspoken together in her dusty belly
moving straw bales undone
by mice over the course of hungry winter.

A noble, grey leviathan creaky and sagging
in every other spot,
she's the static agent of our conveyance
to a shore of destiny we thought
long behind us. Tired and grand
and in cahoots with the pedantic Prankster,
whom the charitable call God,
she takes care of us
in the old school-mistress style:
good lessons delivered sternly
disguising affection.

Looking back inside
through the gaps in her teeth
from the distance of time,
we'll see just how much we owe her
for the many days spent
in the belly of her tranquil mind.

Greg Kennedy

Sweet

Our house in the suburbs
had a backyard, a front yard—
land—land that was his. My father, a son
of Russian immigrants, poor all their lives
was the first in his family to own property.

No one would mistake his house
for anyone else's. He painted
the foundation a light blue. He laid the stones
of his front walk on a curve, not a straight path like
the other houses, stained them coral pink.

He wanted to plant. For the generations before him
sweetness came only from the flesh of fruit.

Cherry and plum trees flourished near the corner
of the porch, raspberry canes smothered
the east wall of the house in cloying abundance
but his pride was the apple tree that thrived
in the centre of the backyard.

Five types of apples grew on that tree. He pruned it,
fertilized it. Baskets and baskets of apples
we didn't know
what to do with.

Linda Frank

Not Your Garden Variety Stories of the Grand River Watershed

I. Contrapuntal Vision of the Twice-Displaced

We are novice tree planters and gardeners, studying with survivalist zeal the fluvial dips and alluvial turns of the Grand River Watershed. We have followed different routes but our destination is, like yours, a place to put down roots. We two, from distant continents and lands, are grafted into one here, sharing, as we do, the émigré's affliction: the contrapuntal vision of the twice-displaced. Acute awareness of simultaneous dimensions. Blessed and cursed to forever see two lands, two rivers, two of everything (and sometimes even multiples). Where pomelo trees and tamarinds, ginger flower and hibiscus, cast shadows on Colonial Acres, this brashly named suburban landscape, reminding us of other places. What kind of garden does one plant with the double vision of a drunkard?

II. Weather Stories

The weather is a national obsession, so varied and so changeable that weather forecasts evolve to "weather stories." In our saga of transplantation, not just from that southerly place inverted in our liquid-courage memories, but also from our lateral migrations from Montreal to Waterloo, we battle ever colder climes before we reach this Carolinian life zone. We garden in the Saint Lawrence lowlands, taking ancestral cues from my partner's Mayan heritage, planting beans, corn and squash in close companionship. Little do we know this humble trinity bears its own familial name—the Iroquois' "Three Sisters"—along the ancient highway. There must be other weather stories here, telling us of times the Peoples of the south exchanged gardening tips and seeds and meals and close companionship with the Peoples of the north. A time when this great hemisphere, now dismembered like a butchered turkey, was ungated, unmapped and fluid like the rivers that sustain it. If we spend more time listening to these other tales, the weather might appear less all-consuming.

III. And Fruit Abundant

Allah hath promised to Believers, men and women, gardens under which rivers flow, to dwell therein. Have we not arrived in such a place? Is this to be our Jannah, our Garden-Paradise? For so it goes, those admitted here, will be among *trees layered with fruit abundant.* Date-palm, pomegranate, lemon, fig. Such riverine commandments could be mistaken, to a child born in the mirage-laden heat of the Indian subcontinent, for a sign, celestial: All gardens must bear fruit! Apple, pear, peach, cherry, plum seem the obvious choice but, as I come to learn, are transplants, one and all! Imposters! Denizens, like me. So where have all the native fruit-bearers gone? Pawpaw, Chokecherry, Red Mulberry, Wild Grape, Juneberry, Staghorn Sumac. Surely I've seen their arching boughs on the banks of conservation creeks, and the no-trespassing slopes of storm-water drains? Unceremoniously denied the horticulturist's stamp of approval. Tucked out of sight and out of mind in nursery-clearance-bins, marked down with 'buyer beware' labels for their "messy" profiles and "invasive" dispositions. But who is invading whom in these post-lapsarian palimpsests where non-native rivals like European Buckthorn and Crimson Queens wage botanical warfare? One can only hope that hell hath no fury like a fruit tree scorned.

IV. So Much More Than Fifty Shades of Green

As far as this land goes, our learning curve is steep. Far steeper than the arable hills and dandelion lawns of a watershed pastoral. Like Genghis Khan and Catherine Parr Traill, we must tie up the laces of our weather-storied sneakers and walk stealthily, alert, like double agents, both resident and alien. We must catalogue and describe, like Ibn Khaldun or Herodotus before him, everything we see, before we don the gardener's mitt or wield a pair of secateurs. We must make mental registers of our neighbours' gardens in the effort to adapt, acculturate, blend in. But the drunkard's double vision is playing tricks on us again. The contrapuntal lens of the twice-displaced has left us colour-blind and all we see is fifty shades of green, green, green. We crave, like hunger artists, the palette of that other place with its saturated pigments. Thankfully, the story's always changing where nothing is as it first appears: Blue Beech, White Spruce, Black Walnut, Green Ash, Black Oak, Yellow Birch, Silver Maple, White Pine. And like the capillary-red willow roots bursting through the banks of the Grand River, we feel our pulse, we catch our breath, we rest. At home. At last.

Mariam Pirbhai

Controlled Burn: Phragamites

A bobby pin.

Fire tearing sideways through the raspberries.

A bobcat
in the rounded moss humps
feline charcoal.

is an invasive plant causing damage to Ontario's biodiversity, wetlands and beaches

Flannel flames gust,
a heat that climbs its own shoulders to jump.

is rooting to extreme lengths, allowing it to survive in relatively dry areas

John Owen Lynch's eldest girl
had another inside her, skeletonized.

is a perennial grass that has been damaging ecosystems in Ontario for decades

Every hydro pole along the Blair Road a perfect arrow of yellow.
An outward-rolling rim of scorch.

is not clear how it was transported to North America from its native home in Eurasia

Boiled tongues are licking
the residential grid, the flammable golf course surface.

is an aggressive plant that spreads quickly and out-competes native species for water and nutrients.

At the riverbank
the controlled burn dives
straight down into the shale—

a half-life of 5568 years
clocks to ash at 14 minutes and
8 seconds.

is releasing toxins from its roots into the soil to hinder the growth of and kill surrounding plants

The hands on Andrew's stopwatch melt at—

Turkey foot
Little blue stem
Indian grass

The big ash is coming down.

Karen Houle

Somehow, Potatoes

Somehow, the potatoes surprised me. Everything else in this square plot unfurls tentacles of vine and stem in full view: sudden weighted droplets of tomatoes, green-tied to stake; peppers that plainly overweight the stem; long draperies of squash blossoms melting yellow to ground. You can't miss it. Unless you do.

But potatoes? A subterranean impossibility it seemed to me. I followed instruction: diced eyes dropped into dug trough and covered all. But is that all? My first garden, so it's growing whole firsts with wonder each week but none that equals the delight of found potatoes at summer's end hiding beneath mounded shelter, dirt-piled in disbelief.

Under July's blanket of heat, I clawed soil under nail, scraping for *solanum* spuds, hungry for confirmation. When nothing poured through the fingers of space except soil and worm, all the mounding and the watering that came after were acts of faith, or something approaching oh-well-what-the-hell resignation. Fruitless, seedless, I assumed.

But before the sudden dieback; before those thick, stalky greens lost fibrous power in the night's shade of August; before the sunk heart and the despairing shovel thrust; before the leveraged pry of the spade spilt dirtfalls like a bucket excavator and big clods of blanched spuds thudded and rolled out in the sifted light of the sun; before that catch in my breath, a cough of delight, at such unexpected bounty, watch: the midsummer monarchs alight for a minute on the pencil weight of the potato flowers. Potato flowers, you say? Somehow, yes.

Geoff Martin

Healing our Harrowing

We've tilled
till we can't;
now the soil,
elementarily confused,
is more air
than earth;
all its dead and rotting
traits ploughed up
and set against us
in a bipolar heaven
increasingly hot and irksome.

We've tilled
till we can't;
now the soil,
bandaged with plastic,
sweats beneath
its suffocated weeds
crazed by an inaccessible
itch impossible to scratch.

We've tilled
till we can't;
our fields far too well travelled:
downstream from the farm
leaving sandy, salty beaches
behind.

We've tilled
till we can't;
and a question gets planted
in this desert:

will we be
as diligent and determined
in our healing
as in our harrowing?

Greg Kennedy

FOOD

"If we acknowledged that everything we consume is the gift of Mother Earth,we would take better care of what we are given."

—Robin Wall Kimmerer

"The Serviceberry: An Economy of Abundance"[44]

[44] From Robin Wall Kimmerer, "The Serviceberry: An Economy of Abundance," *Emergence Magazine*, Oct. 26, 2022.

Eat the Love[45]

To be Real People
We humans have a need
To feed our bodies regularly
To keep our spacesuits clean and functioning well
As they house our true nature—
That place within us
That comes from another
And will one day take its place among the stars

Know that when we talk about food
We are just talking about life
When we take in that which we call food
We are taking in the forces of our cosmic family.
Eat the Love.

It could have been different.
We could fill up at stations like gasoline
For fuel
Stick a nozzle in our armpit and be on our way.
Or, plug a three-prong in our bellybutton
To recharge our batteries.
Instead
We get to
Gather and pick and chop and slice and sip and share and husk and
grind and stir and salivate
In anticipation … and savor …

45 This piece comes from the Introduction to Chandra Maracle's current PhD work, entitled "A Family Affair: Exploring a Haudenosaunee Relationship to Food."

This is our inheritance
This is our birthright
So little asked in return
Dance
Sing
Enjoy
Repeat
So before we begin to talk
About food matters, issues and concerns
I acknowledge you, as an eater
One who chooses life
With every spoonful.

Chandra Maracle

If You Know Apples

If you know apples you know
that a McIntosh bunches up
to its stem, swells so close
it nearly touches, you'd never
mistake it for a Spartan,
shaped like a bowl at its navel,
that the flesh of a Spy is
tinged amber, like leaves
after frost, that a Talman
Sweet is not sweet but
unique like an old Appal-
achian woman who is wholly
herself, when you cut apples
crosswise, you find the part
you don't eat, the star holding
seeds, a star at the heart of
all apples.

If you know apples
you know it was October
when the snake spoke
leaves burning primary red
maple scenting each breath
exile and sin unconceived, it was
October and Eve only wanted that
crisp spray on her palate
the star in white flesh
the starfull of seeds

plump mystery in her palm.

Marilyn Gear Pilling

Rhubarb

Sit any longer staring out the window like this you'll probably catch them at it.
Budging up from the ground of their own half-moon bed (that fast!)
not even waiting to shuck off the last shawl of snow before

nudging those rose-pink nubbins unspeakably private publicly up through
the soil and snow and the stalks of last year's patch, a kind of comic-
strip tease resurrection to illustrate the day. Or growth made

visible *in camera* out in the hidden wide. A 19th century don in his black drape
squinting camera-eyed at the common young could not be more voyeur.
There is something scandalous about pink. Yet you sit and spy

on these striplings turning to strapping ados, to pushy nextbed neighbours. Extra
year extra shove, colony on the climb, persistent, faithful to the point of
invasive. Never mind. Keep them. Move the extras to another

patch of garden bed; you'll be wanting all of it when you make *rosée*. I didn't
mention *la rosée de rhubarbe*? Ah. Best-kept secret. For another day.
If it's rhubarb resurgence this must be maple syrup season. Yes:

Michel has already dropped off your delirious cans of first run, whose trees you
can almost see from here; you know the taste of that first sap rising from
Ontario side-roads and the old-order spigots the Mennonites

sold you though the new way's tube and vacuum festoon Michel's *boisé*. Never mind.
We're using up the planet but we'll go out loving it. Or we'll learn from it
before it's too late: one or the other. We'll eat till we die.

I'm not suggesting starvation. Once I saw a bug chawing on a leaf while all the
while another bigger bug chawed on his body from behind.
I hope I haven't spoiled your lunch.

Rhubarb is of course bitter but with maple syrup it is ambrosia. Now pink
springs eternal you can gorge on your freezers' supplies of rose-tinted
mini-dice you laid up last year. You'll barely finish that feast

before you're dicing up this year's garden. Feasts to die for. But don't.
Live a bit longer, sitting by the fire, staring out the window at the last
snow, watching the rhubarb surge, waiting till it's time,

taking Patience Gray for your model: patience: *Honey from a Weed*
on your lap never gone out of print since she wrote it three decades ago.
Living that close to the source.

Mia Anderson

For my Friend Who Grows Peaches

I stopped by to trade
a poem for a peach
knowing these hurried words
are culls
useless as the shock of waste
to you, riding
down aisles of old earth
your wrinkled fingers wrapped
round the wheel of the world
understanding the demands
of soil, limb
sky, leaf
and seasonal relations
with living things

you with the feel of
a peach in your hand
full round, easily
bruised like marriage
whose bloom comes away
on your fingers
when you grasp too tight
a peach cradled
in your long hand
a planet in the air
it was born to

It's a matter of timing
of predictable surprises
winter kill, blossom set
parasitic infestation
drought and canker
pick and pack and
come inside
proud of your acquaintance
with the secret life of trees
suspicious of the return
of other verities

So I'll keep my poem
and eat the silent fruit
you hand me

David Haskins

Food Chains (for Cathie)

I can't kill spiders anymore,
find it increasingly difficult
to think bacon and eat pig,
wonder at pastel egg yolks
and remember that at least
Aunt Rose's chickens ran loose
under her porch and trees,
work so hard at denying
the obvious connections
that the subtler connections
between my hamburger
and someone else's starvation
run headless under the porch
of my ambivalence, trailing blood.

Last summer I waited for my sister
in front of a turkey plant,
fighting the stench as white
feathers blew past free
and useless. There was time
to count the cages on the semis
that kept pulling up: 500 a load.
A white coat walked by and said,
"One hour from truck to butterball.
They never know what hits them."

That's why I can't kill spiders
anymore. I know what hits them.

But if the problem were that simple
I could be a vegetarian
in an infested house.

Eating dismembered plants.

The radio says government
health standards allow
for a certain level
of insect parts in flour,
bread, cereal, et cetera.
I pictured an inspector
watching the packaging of a field,
grain and creatures caught
in the fist of machinery—
the inspector's checkmarks
shaped like buglegs.

Too much sensitivity
is unfitting me for life.
Living requires eating requires death.
But does it require cruelty,
waste, disrespect or ignorance
of the weight of our link…
this link the earth is wearing
like a noose?

Bernadette Rule

Good Bones

Inside the can of salmon
a fragment of skeleton
lifts out whole
its pop-bead spine holding
despite all that's happened
in its cruel afterlife,
a scrap here and there
of silver chainmail

Rib bones sweep downward
on either side like ivory combs
This brilliant mechanism
that swept the flat body of the fish
so supplely through the changing
chambers of its world—an answer
to water—now thrown onto the compost
with a prayer for forgiveness

Bernadette Rule

Roma

Up the gravel track from Springbank Farm
the tomatoes in the community garden
sag and shine equally, heavy after a big lunch of summer.
They watch the leaves of North Dumfries turn colour
'til the ball diamond at Eby Crest Park lights up,
then they turn in for the night.

Midnight of the autumn solstice, cloud hands
slip around the moon's watchful face.
Covering her eyes and mouth, in one fluid motion
the fog-blade slides from its hiding place
in the buckthorn hedgerow,
and, as it is written, *lays waste.*

At dawn, snuffed out candle-smoke
spirals up from the fruiting bodies, stalk stiff
in the mud on either side of the quake boards.

The Roma stand together in a fatalized field, staring outwards.
Their lace-green skirts are charred at the edges, curling up.
At their feet: a perfect ring, a clutch of cold red eggs,
silent as the story she won't speak anymore.

Down the hill from the slaughter, the henhouse
awakes; hands reach underneath female
fluff for everyday miracles.

Everyday miracles are revealed. They are in the dented straw,
shaped like a mother's body, warm and edible.

Even the plainest hen will gather herself, and step, and step
out a stamp-sized door onto grass chalked with hoarfrost.

The vegetable mothers, though, the ones who sleep rough in the open field:
their eggs are stone cold. Most have split open
in the head from the high drop out of her arms.
Others show bruises where Jack Frost pressed his thumbs
into the fontanel until the pink pulse of flesh stopped
flickering at the edge. Those ones look like tiny unborn lepers.

A hypothermic injection into plump veins, all at once
an entire family goes black and slack.

The ones that look like they are only sleeping are not sleeping.
They have already been entered from the dirt side by earwigs and
gluey slugs—
black slivers of wriggling tubes are sucking the sweet flesh
into their own horrible little adventitious bodies.

At first light, I find myself walking up and down the rows
of the badly marred and newly dead, gathering them up
in dainty salvage, bulging my hoodie pouch.

By the time I cross the farmhouse lintel more have died
and bled right through to my stomach skin.

At the kitchen sink, with her old hooked knife, I pare away
the surface damage, the canker rot, then drown what's left to drown:
the marmorated stink bugs and the slugs hiding out in the good parts:

I make plain tomato sauce—
Salsa di pomodori.

We eat it for dinner that same night,
on pasta, with nothing but fresh ground black pepper.

Karen Houle

Pruning Black Raspberries

Last year's canes droop
in a tangle away from the fence
their bark stripped by winter
old fruit clusters left unpicked.

Last summer's yellow-jackets
sucked the purple sugar
sparrows punctured fat seeds
and left the bleeding berries
to rot in the sun that ripened them.

Woody stalks crack limp in the shears;
a few soft stems with split buds
barely hint at new harvest
free to first takers.

Their persistence to reassert themselves
despite disease, destruction, and death
to fulfill their role year after year
with only a little discipline from
someone with a pair of secateurs.

Hard to imagine being without them
a promise broken, a faith betrayed
but wasps and birds will migrate
to apples and pears, and soon
we will revisit these plants
that once covered the naked fence
with branch, leaf and fruit
ever something to anticipate.

David Haskins

White Berries

Alyssa plants strawberries
in a garden plot as big
as a bathtub. If it were
(a bathtub), and I lay down

those feathered leaves would grow
between my toes. I would squeeze,
juice the woodland berries. But

"There'll be no fruit this summer," Alyssa
says. "First, the plant gets stronger."

Fragaria vesca, native. Drought
tolerant. Partially shaded. It grows no flower,
no fruit for a year and neither
do I. The seed sits one inch deep and
my basement apartment about eight feet,
but when the timing is right
we both feel the sun.

When berries come, they ripen
but no one—human or squirrel—can tell.
White as a wishbone, big as a child's
thumbnail, they bend their stems. Quiet. I
pluck, taste, and we both dissolve. Cotton
candy squish, tongue to mouth-roof
pressing, soft, gone, puckerless.

Soon they escape. Leaves and runners
reach gardens we did not plant; neighbours
reap. What a shame. To see, to eat
without the wait.

Elise Arsenault

We're Not Worried

Danish astronomers have just discovered sugar

—simple molecules of glycolaldehyde—floating
in the gas around a young, sun-like star, four hundred
light years away. The molecules are falling
toward
a binary star, a system of two bodies,
one
primary, one companion, orbiting about
a common centre of mass. This space sugar, they think,
helps replicate DNA. We too orbit. Tonight

it's ice cream at The Boathouse Tea Room, noticing where
the Speed River's melting and, more urgently, the sides
of cones. We choose chocolate and vanilla, measure
the deviations. An old lady is feeding geese.

Astronauts wanted neapolitan for their trips
to the moon. Freeze-dried prototypes proved impractical.
Crumbs were dangerous to microgravity, like bird

parts in plane engines. Now they sell it at the NASA
gift shop, so we can all travel to outer space too.

There are more choices than stars. Scientists are making
breakthroughs in slowing down melt, though can't make it healthy.

You can't take sugar out because of the role it plays
The chemical structure girds against dismantlement[46]

Madhur Anand

---

46 Lines adapted from an article by Susan Burton in *New York Magazine* entitled "Chemistry in a Cone." [Author's note.]

Evan Said

In the near future we will grow food vertically.
The condo bubble in Toronto must explode first.

Suds, sofas, coffeemakers, and dreams will be mopped up.
Glass towers higher than First Canadian Place

will be filled up with light, whole wheat, and arugula.
There will be machinations, of course. Like where to put

the cows. The bankers will enjoy their occupations.
And I will still want this: strangers to read these poems.

Madhur Anand

Mennonite Wife Prayer: Chokecherry

The pucker, the rusted bucket pings, a ringing,
Plucks the ripeness free, the ladder steadied, and then the sourest singing.

The hymnal, it's the humming of her Enoch, a bitterness, a waxwing.
The milking time each morning, it's rickety limbs, and then the rough unstringing.

Dear Lord:

There is some fruit.
Here are my hands.
My hands are touching the fruit,
Making accidental music in the branches.

Forgive me.

Karen Houle

FUTURE PERFECT TENSE

"Our major crises—pandemics, climate disruption and biodiversity loss—all have rootsin our lack of recognition of our place in nature. We can and must do better."

—David Suzuki[47]

"*We're made from this stuff*; this earth, this shale, this mud and suffering clay."

—John Terpstra[48]

[47] David Suzuki, "Science Matters" online, April 9, 2021.

[48] John Terpstra, *Falling into Place* (Gaspereau, 2002).

Hail

Hello from inside
the albatross
with a windproof lighter
and Japanese police tape.
Hello from staghorn
coral beds
waving at the beaked whale's
mistake,
all six square metres
of fertilizer bags.
Hello from can-opened
delta gators,
taxidermied
with twenty-five grocery sacks
and a Halloween Hulk mask.
Hello from the zipped-up
leatherback
who shat bits of rope for a month.
Hello from bacteria
making their germinal way
to the poles in the pockets
of packing foam.
Hello from low-density
polyethylene dropstones
glacially tilled
by desiccated,
bowel-obstructed camels.
Hello from six-pack rings
and chokeholds,
from breast milk
and cord blood,
from microfibres
rinsed through yoga pants

and polyester fleece,
biomagnifying predators
strafing the treatment plants.
Hello from acrylics
in G.I. Joe.
Hello from washed up
fishnet thigh-highs
and frog suits
and egg cups
and sperm.
Hello.

Adam Dickinson

Psalm 46

How on earth do we square them:
a faith in creative goodness
and the acidic evidence
that Creation is thoroughly screwed?
Beneath the rainbow covenant
that stretches like fallout
over the post-diluvial world
sea-levels, like maggots, creep up
reversing by inches the Genesis timeline,
sending old Noah nervously back to his toolshed.
The City of God, is it sustainable?
Does it sit too heavily on the fields
and flowers of the Promised Land?
Are its citizens oily slickers
who can't tell an elm tree from an oak?

Still, our Creator lives
and we are the living proof
even in our decadence.

Come and see the Wonders of the World,
and I don't mean the pyramids
or Machu Picchu.
Get out of the plane and onto the ground
bend down
and study a square foot of forgotten earth.
There's mundane magic most marvellous
moving around:
living proof our Creator lives
despite our slow-motion, repeat-loop
Fall.

Greg Kennedy

The Day the Earth Cried

The Earth cried yesterday
And no one listened

They saw but they didn't care
They knew but they didn't stop

They watched, they were appalled
but they watched
They filed letters, they said excuse me
that's wrong

They told their friends, this is wrong
And the friends said yes this is wrong

And the government said it will be okay
And the people said, yeah maybe so

And the Earth cried
And the people watched

And hurricanes happened
And the weather turned treacherous

And the Earth cried
And the people watched

The oceans and seas turned against man
Everywhere in the world weather
attacked man

And the Earth cried

And the people watched

And one day the people died

And the Earth cried and nobody watched.

Gimaa (Chief) R. Stacey Laforme

The Egg as Immigrant

Eggshells were the earliest suitcases,
carefully packed bags.

Homesick had its shape:
one end less eager than the other,
broadening downward,
an album of wet plans
opened and pored over.

How long does it take to say
that you have always been here?

Mammals thrust their eggs
deep within warm inland flesh,
as if to renounce the struggle
of their own immigration,
thin and humble luggage that once salted them
with scales.

The egg moves in humans now
like creeks filled and buried in the centres of cities,
their passages jerked to the network of sewers.

It travels once a month
in the fertile interval lands;
the blood that emerges, also pushed underground,
unspoken.

***

Gravity, the egg-shapes of rain
uncommitted to the sky.

We arrive holding on
to where we've been:
          into any gushing wound,
you can pump seawater
and a body will continue to live.

Toward what new land will something yet
compose its shell

and climb out of our moisture,
the shape of its doubt
unevenly glistening at the edges of our eyes?

Adam Dickinson

The Kind of World We Live In

—lines for Lent

The kind of world we live in
is fraught
with where and when the next outbreak
will occur
which passenger aircraft
the missile will hit
whether the children will be freed
from their cages
to go find their mothers and fathers, if they can
and what we'll all do next
after the last iceberg has melted
into the waters that lap against our e-car doors

The kind of world we live in
feels as though it's reaching a pitch
and here I sit
cinching up the hiking boots
for another forty-day wilderness trek
another round
of walking over rock
talking to trees
and hoping for blessed nothing to happen
while I'm out there alone

The world is on your shoulders
it's in your backpack
which just happens to get lighter and lighter
the farther you go
the deeper you delve into these woods
the closer you come
to losing it all
for love
of the kind of world we live in

while fasting on
the roots and berries of wild hope

John Terpstra

Climate Change?

The truth of the land is a long and difficult journey,
but it is past time it was told

The land needs a voice, for though
she speaks, we do not listen

We need to remember our creation and hers
and the link that exists

A link that was forged when your ancestors
first placed foot upon her

It is a link that cannot be broken,
no matter the time or generations that pass

Whether it is a living, breathing connection
and part of your daily life

Or if it exists buried behind walls of apathy,
greed or ignorance it is still there

It can be celebrated, or it can remain hidden
behind self-delusion

But it can never be disconnected

So listen, learn, understand our Mother the Earth
and then maybe we can give her voice

If not, we doom our children to chaos

We do the one thing that every parent swears
upon the birth of their child
they will never do

Take away their right to a future

We as parents swear a silent oath that
we will give our life to protect our children

Yet we are all culpable

I do not have the answers,
for they require more than I

Perhaps I can offer a place to begin

Instead of thinking that climate change
is a problem to be solved

Think instead of Mother Earth
as a soul to be saved

If we can do this simple thing
we can change everything.

Gimaa (Chief) R. Stacey Laforme

How to Love a Landfill

Sink yourself down into the wetland
and stay awhile.

Imagine the love you felt
when you gathered up the dog to have her cremated

And then put your ear down deep against the silt
of the Late Wisconsinan Wentworth Till

Attend to the task of imagining;
it all needs to be imagined

The mallards rasping overhead
and the white tatting of wild strawberry flowers

The lace-boned frame of swamp milkweed
its white sap memoried into name

Strike a tuning fork against a rock and hold it
up to the ear of a blossom

Fill your vial with a fine yellow film of sounds
or pick up your paint brush and dust the pollen into fruiting.

If you make your bed with the glacial meltwater at your heels,
curl into the deep ribs of bedrock, pull up a blanket of earth

The land we have come to accept as a hill
may begin to know you; it may at last roll over
and call you by name.

Anna Bowen

Heaven

It rains all night and in the morning every blossom
is exalted, every tendril of June vegetation
infuses the air; the earth itself
smells new. In walking shoes and winded
by the hill, I hear a rich, full-throated *Heaven*
sung forth. Two notes. They come
from on high, have heft, yet rest upon the air.
It comes again, four notes this time:
I'm in Heaven. A tall man standing,
straddling the ridge of a steep roof. Hammer
in hand, body relaxed. It's apparent that
yes, he is in heaven, and that's
a good thing because Joseph Campbell says
that if you don't get heaven here,
you won't get it anywhere.
And now I'm in heaven, seeing him, in heaven,
and turn south onto Paradise Road—yes, truly—
and here's another man, on a step ladder, creating
an eternal face of brick in a pattern
of running bond for a small house,
and he's in heaven too,
his left hand loading just the right amount
of mortar onto his trowel, the risen sun
blessing his bare back.
The wind within carries me along the road,
honey and milk are on my tongue
and my feet skirt the potholes of Paradise Road,
their brimmed offerings of tree and sky—

the three of us, getting it here.

Marilyn Gear Pilling

Spiral of the Cosmos

Loyola House, Guelph

Here the whole cosmos is pressed onto the land,
in this spiral that tells the great history of time.
I begin at the centre, enfolded in a kernel, and gyre

myself out through all that has been, through all
the orders of being that surround me now.
Here millennia are taken at a stride,

and I walk as a giant in the field of time.
This is the kindergarten of the cosmos,
a first lesson in the intricate ribboning of creation.

I walk the billions of years of becoming,
trace the sinuous path from origin to here.
It is eons before life becomes visible to my eyes.

I follow in slow contemplative steps
the wish of what is to keep remaking itself,
to indulge in, elaborate, the nearly unimaginable

patience of invention. Photos remind me
of the instances here: the insects and frogs,
the snakes and birds, the padding mammals,

the flowers pouring their colours on this land.
In my spiralling steps I keep meeting the twisting
of cataclysms into new species, this resilience,

---

[49] On the grounds of Loyola House in Guelph, the Stations of the Cosmos is a spiral that traces the history of the universe from its origin to the present, with plaques of text and photos that mark key moments of the process, allowing one to walk, on land, the course of the cosmos. [Author's note.]

this insistent imperative to become something more.
I trace this elementary narrative I barely know,
that I should have been told at the knees of the world,

feel how it fits the gaping of my life.
I am rejoined with my pre-human selves
in swirling of matter, in fish and amphibian,

in all the long animal lineage of my flesh.
How late an arrival I am to this pageant,
how brief the few words my species has spoken,

how unbearable all the loss that we risk.
All history in an hour, all being in my body,
and I am this one tiny tentacle of creation.

I end in the present unbounded moment,
at this precise holy juncture of the story
that discloses my place in the magnitude of things.

I emerge to this land and its local magic,
know it as plainly sacred ground,
am born here and born here as if it were home.

Brian Day

Haiku Series

after brief rain
a rainbow over
the Grand River

above the Mountain
a red balloon rises
no string attached

winding trail
behind a haunted house
calls from unknown birds

on the sunset lake
a snowy egret takes off
the other not in sight

fog lifts
a thrush's song
through the woods

maple trees
along the Bruce trail
Thompson's vibrant paintings

shaking off more snow
the icy willow echoes
spring, spring

Anna Yin

beyond the fridge[50]

in the 5 a.m. dark a man pushes a cart to Cedar street & squashing his cigarette on the sidewalk, he shuffles up some stairs towards a wooden shed & opens a fridge stocked with honeycrisp & fruit cups & tin cans stacked neatly in rows & content, he fills his cart with what he needs to share a meal with friends & later that afternoon a mother & daughter bring dense & sweet ma'amoul to the fridge & remember the kindness of strangers that sustained their flight from famine & violence & the market expands then contracts & the fridge, luminescent under haloed moonset, stands briefly barren until a restaurateur rolls up to unload pre-packaged meals & as i clean a spill inside the fridge i wonder if this is enough & it's not perfect but hungry people gots to eat & folks gots food to give & maybe this is how we plant seeds to grow something better & isn't it true that ideas like this new-old ice box get us to make moves for community & isn't this how we might create momentum to abolish hunger & dismantle the structures of poverty & build a better world from this communal ground?

Fitsum Areguy

[50] First presented in an art installation mounted in the summer of 2023, on the side of a painted shipping container along the Gaukel Block pop-up pedestrian street in Kitchener. [Author's note.]

Sequoyah

If pointed redwoods could walk the land
they might cut the sky into pages
upon which we could read what the stars write
over and over   like school children.

I want to read each page of sky
beneath which I have been honoured to live.
And I want to read the thoughts of my people
beautiful as the stars.

The words of our mouths, written
will rise
            still rooted in our hearts
            and touch the sky.

Bernadette Rule

POETS IN PLACE

responses to three questions about place, grounding, and poetry

Madhur Anand

1. How would you describe your ***relationship to the land****, and how long have you called a particular physical place 'home'?*

I have not thought too consciously about my relationship to land, to be honest, in terms of this land or that land. I have spent most of my life in southern Ontario, but I have lived/travelled in so many different parts of the world. I have studied ecosystems/land as diverse as deserts, tropical forests, boreal landscapes, and Mediterranean wetlands. I have ancestry in Punjab, 'land of five rivers.' However, as an ecological scientist I think I have a different relationship to land than perhaps the average citizen. I see other species, for example, more clearly. I know their natural histories, their interrelations with each other and with us. I also see all that I don't know—Indigenous knowledge, for example.

2. Is your relationship to the land affected by any particular ***religious or spiritual grounding****, or does it come from a* ***specific worldview*** *of any kind?*

I would say my environmental perspective is secular. I am not religious. Having said that, there is a spiritual quality to some of my work in the sense that all poetry is in some way transcendental (going beyond the physical).

I'm very concerned about the status of the world and human impact on the ecosystem, so that does come out in my work. It expresses most sharply the warnings or the concerns—migration, climate change and endangerment of ecosystems.[51]

---

[51] See https://www.therecord.com/life/2015/05/16/professor-marries-science-and-human-experience-in-her-poetry.html

*3. What is your **motivation and hope in writing poetry** related to the environment? What kind of a role do you see poetry as fulfilling?*

The poems reflect my knowledge and my concerns. I consciously include environmental issues in my poetry because I am a professor of environmental sciences, and these issues are part of not only my knowledge base, but also my experience. It's hard to separate them from any other mode of inquiry, including the poetic mode. And I do see my poetry as having a contribution to make to thinking about environmental issues, because it contains scientific knowledge on these issues as well as personal reflections. I do have hope for solutions. I think there is no other way to view things.

Art can change the way we think and the way we behave quite radically, but without a scientific framework it can only go so far in solving environmental problems. It's perhaps because of the longstanding (artificial, unhelpful) divide between art and science in society that we must turn to one another for a mutual response, perhaps a collective one, during times of crisis. But there are similarities: In science, an index is a statistical device used to study complex systems, like ecosystems, economies, the human heart, and climate change. In poetry, the devices are different but many of the systems are the same. Writing poems can represent a critical slowing down, measured by new indexes (such as the "early warning signal") used to discover or predict sudden transitions, like revelations.[52]

Madhur Anand is a professor in the School of Environmental Sciences at the University of Guelph, and the inaugural Director of the Guelph Institute for Environmental Research. Her first book of poetry, *A New Index for Predicting Catastrophes*, was published with McClelland & Stewart in 2015; a second book, *Parasitic Oscillations*, was published in 2022. She is also the author of the experimental memoir *This Red Line Goes Straight to Your Heart*, winner of the 2020 Governor General's Literary Award for Non-Fiction, and has published several other literary works in national and international literary magazines.

---

52 See https://artistsandclimatechange.com/2020/12/23/an-interview-with-madhur-anand-and-kathryn-mockler/

Mia Anderson

1. How would you describe your ***relationship to the land****, and how long have you called a particular physical place 'home'?*

Intense. It always has been, but it has grown over time. Both sets of my grandparents had serious gardens; one of them included food, even chickens. Yet I had to clamour for years before I got a birthday gift of a farm visit. It was to a sheep farm. Who knew I'd end up as a shepherd? And then as an Anglican priest—about whom people joked, Aha! just changed flocks, eh? There's a lot to that, actually; I always felt shepherding was the best analogy, for me anyway, to being a parish priest. I left the theatre (I used to be an actress too) when I wanted to grow things and switch my art form from human to non-human nature. Hence poetry. My husband and I first lived on an experimental farm belonging to the Univ. of Guelph. Sheep again (with bags tied to their butts, to measure their feed conversion efficiency, don'tcha know). We rented the house and were allowed a big garden. I was into growing food, and got serious about black currants. Which is a real investment in land. We thought we'd better put those roots down into our own land, so Tom took a compass and drew a circle around the campus (he taught at U of G) and we bought within a radius he figured he could drive daily, to teach. And the sheep, and the black currants, and a market garden, and a barnful of animals, followed.

When we eventually moved here to Québec for my parish, and then retired to property on the shore of the St Lawrence, the intense relationship to land continued. There's a Celtic concept called 'Thin Places,' which wriggles into my poetry, and I even dare to claim I live in a Thin Place now. I've gotten to know the director of the Office of the Wendat Nation here; I wanted to learn if anyone had lived on my precise piece of land before. You'd be right if 'people of the land' comes to mind—for me a deeply moving biblical phrase—and very apt for First Nations too. (The Wendat are called 'farmers of the north'.) It's about 19 years now that I've been joined at the hip to this piece of land. They will have to drag me off. And oh, they may, they may.

2. Is your relationship to the land affected by any particular ***religious or spiritual grounding****, or does it come from a* ***specific worldview*** *of any kind?*

I'm feeling my way to understanding this, but I'd say it's the other way round: my relationship to the land affects my spiritual grounding. Back to Thin Places. To put it wildly simply, the concept is that certain actual, material, geographical places are particularly thinly veiled from the immaterial or spiritual. Many accounts bear this specificity out. Yet I hesitatingly begin to think that *any* intentional, let's call it *participation*, in the land, the land's life, can bring about a thinning of that veil. Part of what I'm saying is that *land teaches*. Land, and its inhabitants, *reveal*: life forms, and rocks, and soil, and waterflow. I know there is a label out there: 'natural theology,' and I simply will not ever know if I would have arrived where I am now or not, absent Christian 'revelation,' nor which is chicken and which is egg.

3. What is your ***motivation and hope in writing poetry*** *related to the environment? What kind of a role do you see poetry as fulfilling?*

I honour the intimations of etymology: poetry is our handiwork. We make things. I am clearer and clearer these days that 'bearing witness' is the function it performs—at least for me. Gesticulating towards something and saying, "That-there! Look!" I think the passion to do that is becoming stronger—probably as I get older and have less time to bear witness. But why do it? Maybe as simple as Handel replying to a question about writing Messiah. He is said to have said something like, "I wrote it to make people better." I will hazard this: "I write to make people fall in love, with that, there, this"—or, to be accurate to what my perception declares—"You." 'You' is the name I give to gesticulation's that, there, this. For me, poetry is a form of theology. It is god-talk, and if (as I'm hinting) land is how God hides, then land-talk is god-talk: the ineffable hiding in plain sight, kitted out in a glorious costume disguise of his own making. As a poem of mine elsewhere begins:

> Physics is how God hides.
> It's what hides him.
>
> What a brilliant disguise!

If I could woo you into loving it, you might take care of it, you might stand up for soil, for diversity, for regenerative agriculture before it's too late. So I sing, like Teilhard de Chardin, my Hymn to Matter.

Mia Anderson has had six lives; she doesn't yet admit to a seventh. Born in Toronto, many years an actor—Stratford, British & Canadian rep, two one-woman shows, radio and TV—she turned to poetry and shepherding and market gardening, before becoming an Anglican priest. Her parish took her to Québec, after which she and her husband retired to the shores of the *fleuve*, where she has done some translating. She has won two Malahat Long Poem prizes, the National Magazine Award, and the Montreal Prize, and has published seven books of poetry (*Appetite, Château Puits '81, Practising Death, The Sunrise Liturgy, Light Takes, Into This Holy Estate*, and *O is For Christmas*).

Fitsum Areguy

1. How would you describe your ***relationship to the land****, and how long have you called a particular physical place 'home'?*

Other than very brief stints working abroad in Spain and Jeju, the longest I have lived anywhere has been in Southwestern Ontario, specifically in Kitchener. And yet, I often struggle to call this place my home. This feeling of home and dislocation has influenced and shaped my relationship to the land.

When I was young, my father rented a small lot in a community garden. I can't recall exactly where it was located, but I do remember that we passed through the countryside on the way there. My brothers and I liked to spot the horses and cows that punctuated the otherwise monotonous acres of crops. I built a friendship with that garden lot. The soil felt alive under my feet and the air was distinctly cleaner. I loved to pick up dirt and feel it crumble through my fingers. If I wasn't pulling weeds or plucking fruit and vegetables, I was riding my bike. The dirt road by the garden is where I first mastered riding without training wheels.

As I learned more about the histories of the region, my sense of those vast acres of farmland changed. Pastoral scenes turned into landscapes of domination. From an early age I knew it was unjust that there were people who could own obscene amounts of land while my family was limited to a handful of garden soil. I am haunted by histories that reverberate through time and space, something I wrestle with daily in my organizing, research, and writing.

Thus, to have any kind of sustained relationship to the land, I have needed to locate pockets where I can be protected and heal. Over the last decade or so, I have been restoring my relationship to the land through hidden places around the region, by taking trails that weave under and alongside highways, by hiking through nearby parks and forests, and by participating in emergent rituals of potlucks and ceremonies that breathe new life here, both for me and my various communities.

2. Is your relationship to the land affected by any particular ***religious or spiritual grounding****, or does it come from a* ***specific worldview*** *of any kind?*

Despite distancing myself from the church years ago, I recognize that my orientation to the land was profoundly moulded—and in many aspects, fractured—by Christian doctrine. My journey towards healing has come through a deliberate engagement with Black, Afrodiasporic, and Indigenous ways of being and knowing. By embracing these spiritual, intellectual, and political traditions and teachings, I have slowly been repairing the disconnection wrought by a Christian-centric view of dominion over nature; I am attracted now to Christian mysticism, liberation theology, and ecological theology, especially due to their orientation towards the land, nature, and non-human/more-than-human beings. I approach the land as a being with agency, a living, breathing entity that I seek deep and respectful communion with.

3. What is your ***motivation and hope in writing poetry*** *related to the environment? What kind of a role do you see poetry as fulfilling?*

I recently had the good fortune of hearing a talk by Camille Turner, an acclaimed Canadian artist/scholar whose work combines Afrofuturism and historical research. Turner shared insights into her research, such as her uncovering of the history of slave ships built and ballasted along Newfoundland's eastern coast. The same shipwrights who constructed these ships were also among the first builders of the town, erecting many of the early churches. Walking through these churches and looking up into the naves, Turner realized it resembled looking down into the hold of a ship. This realization led to the creation of "Nave," an immersive multimedia installation commissioned by the Toronto Biennial of Art.

Through her art, Turner is able to repair and reclaim connections to the land and histories, while also challenging and subverting colonial narratives. This is at the heart of my own motivation and hope in writing poetry. Not only do poetry and other forms of writing help me work through hurt and trauma lingering from my time in the church, I write and read poetry to trace the contours of what Katherine McKittrick describes as "a Black sense of place"— landscapes, futures, and lifeworlds where I can exist in the Anthropocene.

Fitsum Areguy is a writer and scholar-activist based in Southwestern Ontario. His work has been published in *Briarpatch Magazine, Canadian Dimension, New Sociology, Red Noise Collective*, and *Korea Exposé*, among others. He is the co-founder and project director for *Textile*, a hyper-local arts collective that provides publishing, mentorship, and curation for writers and artists in Waterloo Region, Ontario, particularly those from historically excluded and marginalized groups. Fitsum volunteers at Multicultural Theatre Space and ACCKWA (The AIDS Committee of Cambridge, Kitchener, Waterloo and Area), and in his free time he enjoys playing pick-up ball with strangers and listening to dance music.

Elise Arsenault

1. How would you describe your ***relationship to the land****, and how long have you called a particular physical place 'home'?*

I grew up in the suburbs of Oakville, Ontario. When neighbourhood friends knocked on my door as a kid, it was either to bike to the corner store for candy or to the ponds to catch tadpoles and climb trees. The first birds I knew by name were red-winged blackbirds, and the first time I met a snail was after crushing it. I felt horrible.

Ten years ago I moved to Hamilton, where I feel most at home.

I would say my relationship to the land is growing. I'm learning from friends who know much more about this place than I do. On hikes along the Bruce Trail they pluck the curls of wild grape vines, or the heart-shaped leaves of wood sorrel for me to taste. They yank invasive phragmites and garlic mustard from boulevards, so now I do too.

I feel most peaceful seated somewhere along the Bayfront, or in a hammock between maples at Gage Park. I hope to keep discovering natural spaces in the city with the promise we'll get to know each other better over time.

2. Is your relationship to the land affected by any particular ***religious or spiritual grounding****, or does it come from a* ***specific worldview*** *of any kind?*

My faith is a biblical faith, in that I believe the world was (and is still being) created by a good and present God. Creation reveals his nature: beautiful, startling, holy. I think of the powerful current of Tews Falls, hurling over a fossil-clad rock face. Or the audacity of squirrels. Or the almost galactic beauty of a wild columbine flower.

I think nature and spirituality are alike in that we are immersed whether or not we pay attention, but the good stuff happens when we do.

*3. What is your **motivation and hope in writing poetry** related to the environment? What kind of a role do you see poetry as fulfilling?*

Poetry is an attentive genre. My favourite poems draw so close to their subject, expanding my empathy and curiosity through nearness. I hope to do this too. I hope readers feel seen while also seeing the world with a little more awe.

Elise Arsenault is a writer and musician living on the traditional territories of the Erie, Neutral, Huron-Wendat, Haudenosaunee and Mississaugas, also named Hamilton, Ontario. She holds an MFA in creative nonfiction from the University of King's College. To read and hear her latest work, visit elisearsenault.ca.

Gary Barwin

1. How would you describe your ***relationship to the land****, and how long have you called a particular physical place 'home'?*

I've lived in Hamilton for about 30 years. My background is Ashkenazi Jewish—my grandparents were all born in Lithuania, and they moved before the Holocaust to South Africa. Then my parents in the early '60s left South Africa because of political issues, ended up in Northern Ireland, and then after the start of the Troubles I moved here to Canada, to Ottawa, with them when I was nine. So what is my ancestral home and my ancestral language? I don't have a coherent or stable relationship to a particular place and its culture, so I have collected associations and connections to land and culture and language from my family's movement. When I used to visit Ireland, I had all these Romantic thoughts about the Irish land, but as much as I could look at the green hills and feel full of nostalgia, I was also very aware that that feeling was a construction and I was sort of putting it on because it wasn't my cultural home—my parents just happened to move there and I happened to grow up there. For me, living in Hamilton, Ontario, Canada is always about reckoning my thoughts and my sense of myself and my culture and the world through the particularity of the environment that I'm in. If I go outside in a particular spring and feel joy at spring time, it's this spring at this moment in time, not 100 years ago in the Lithuania of my grandparents. I think of Hamilton as "chosen place," and in my relationship to land I'm constantly rediscovering it and creating it for myself. I'm naively noticing that "oh, I'm in this land at this moment surrounded by these trees," and what a beautiful and also absurd thing this is.

2. Is your relationship to the land affected by any particular ***religious or spiritual grounding****, or does it come from a* ***specific worldview*** *of any kind?*

Within the Jewish tradition, except for ideas about Israel as "the land" and returning to Jerusalem, the tradition hasn't been about deeply connecting to a specific place. Jews found themselves always in exile, and I don't want to be an exile. I could claim I'm an exile from Ireland or from Eastern Europe, but I know those were only contingent places. I live in my land and my life and I don't live in exile from my life, so I want to be grounded in place. There's a psychological immanence or presence of the place where I live that connects me and how I move through the land and how I live my days.

In Judaism there is also this sense of layers behind reality, and all sorts of mystic Presences of the Divine in the moment and behind the moment. I don't literally believe that there's really a reality behind reality, but it's so beautiful a vision and so tempting and such a meaningful way to think. It's so seductive and mesmerizing and powerful, and whether one believes in religious traditions or not, it is an incredibly powerful metaphorical expression of the range of what we can possibly feel as humans. There's a deep spiritual sense of the possibility in the world, but I would also say it's the possibility of absurdity.

3. What is your ***motivation and hope in writing poetry*** *related to the environment? What kind of a role do you see poetry as fulfilling?*

I'm engaged in many kinds of poetry that have different functions, and there can be different functions within the same work. Some of my poetry is poetry of witness, where I'm just talking about what exists and what is happening. A really basic role of writers is to speak back to society, and for me I am very specifically speaking back to patriarchal capitalism and its relationship to the environment, because it's destructive and pernicious and pervasive. Writing is one of the ways to provide different ways of seeing, and I guess that provision really is my primary purpose. I've increasingly begun to think about the way in which my Jewish tradition is a religion based on questioning, raising questions rather than having answers, and I would say that kind of opening up of discussion is my aesthetic as an artist.

Gary Barwin is a writer, composer, and multidisciplinary artist. He is the author of 30 books, including *Nothing the Same, Everything Haunted: The Ballad of Motl the Cowboy*, which won the Canadian Jewish Literary Award, was shortlisted for the Vine Award, and was chosen for *Hamilton Reads 2023*. His national bestselling novel *Yiddish for Pirates* won the Leacock Medal for Humour and the Canadian Jewish Literary Award, was a finalist for the Governor General's Award for Fiction and the Scotiabank Giller Prize, and was long-listed for *Canada Reads*. His 2022 poetry collection *The Most Charming Creatures* won the Canadian Jewish Literary Award. His latest book is *Imagining Imagining: Essays on Language, Identity and Infinity*. In Fall 2024, *Scandal in the Alphorn Factory, New & Selected Fiction 1984-2024* was published by Assembly Press. A PhD in music composition, he has been writer-in-residence and taught at many universities, colleges and libraries. In the summer 2023, his permanent public art installation (created with Tor Lukasik-Foss and Simon Frank) *be:longing*, a series of ten bronze sculptures, was installed in Hamilton, Ontario. He lives in Hamilton and at garybarwin.com

Anna Bowen

1. How would you describe your ***relationship to the land****, and how long have you called a particular physical place 'home'?*

I've lived in Guelph for about 10 years, and I was farming here one season before that, but I'm a first-generation Canadian settler so my ancestry isn't part of this land. My relationship to the land has been intentional in that most of the art and poetry I'm involved in tries to make gestures of care to the land because the dominant culture here in Canada, the one I inherit, doesn't exist in a culture of care for the natural world at all. But my relationship is only germinal, a beginner relationship that I still feel is just scraping the surface, even when I've intentionally done projects about land with artists and with writing. As a white settler, a first-generation Canadian, I don't have a lot to draw on with regards to relating to this non-human world in a reciprocal way. I feel that any gestures of care and reciprocity that I'm making fall short, though maybe it's just being a child in the relationship.

2. Is your relationship to the land affected by any particular ***religious or spiritual grounding****, or does it come from a* ***specific worldview*** *of any kind?*

I went to a Christian evangelical summer camp, so a lot of my spiritual formation happened in nature. Even though the sacredness of what was around you wasn't integrated into the teachings in a way that feels sufficient to me, it was present to me. It's not enough for me to say a tree shows me, for example, how I'm rooted in God (as a metaphor)—I want more than that for my spirituality. I can see how the context of climate change and being exposed in my work to Indigenous cosmologies and Indigenous artists pushes me beyond the place of being satisfied with an understanding of the natural world as creation, or just as metaphor for human experience. I would rather engage with an Eastern White cedar as a sentient sacred being, acknowledging what it does and what its relationship to people and animals and the ecosystem around it is, and our interconnectedness. It seems as though settler-colonial cultures are just realizing in the last fifty years what an immense poverty viewing humans as the pinnacle of the natural world represents, how destructive and dangerous it is. And I don't necessarily need to throw the baby out with the bathwater; I think the overarching Christian story of forgiveness and grace I can get behind, and I can see that reflected in the natural world as well.

3. What is your ***motivation and hope in writing poetry*** *related to the environment? What kind of a role do you see poetry as fulfilling?*

People that I work with are very cautious about the word "hope," feeling that it's a type of veneer that causes us to rush too quickly to a conclusion, and that there's a lot of suffering to feel before you move beyond it to hope. I haven't thought through that yet, but to say "where's your hope?" is a trigger for some of those people—it will turn them right off in terms of their experience of Indigenous issues and environmental issues. But poetry is, hopefully, something that can help you sit with discomfort with suffering, sit with injustice without trying to fix it or solve it or make it feel better. I think poetry hopefully enables a kind of mindfulness, and it can use language in a way that is refreshing and provide us with a different access point into our imagination.

Anna Bowen (she/her) is a Guelph, Ontario-based poet, editor, and writer. She holds an MA (2007) from OISE/University of Toronto in Sociology and Equity Studies in Education, with a focus on critical race theory and women and gender studies. She has collaborated with visual artists on projects related to space, care labour, landscape, and access, including Aislinn Thomas' *three windows described by three voices [...]* (2018) and *a convex minutely puckered surface could be called a vertical sea* (2019), and durational installation *Re:Mediate* (2014-2016, published by Publications Studio Guelph) with Christina Kingsbury. She is currently working on poetry that examines reciprocity and relationship with four specific trees; her poetry collection *Holding Places* was published in 2024 from Glove Box Press, and includes “Eastern White Cedar” and “Fossil Wood” from this anthology. She is an editor with ArtsEverywhere.ca and Publication Studio Guelph, and works for the arts foundation Musagetes.

Klyde Broox (1957-2024)

1. How would you describe your ***relationship to the land****, and how long have you called a particular physical place 'home'?*

Grounded in geography of physical location, my poetic practice dubs daily life into poetry to dub poetry into daily life and perform poems as public art, articulating discourses derived from narratives of influential interplay between persons and places. Since birth, I have regarded the entire island of Jamaica, and the African continent, as home. However, in Canada, only Hamilton feels like home to me. Looking across at Hamilton and beyond, as well as within, "Window to a Lake," set in Burlington, my first Canadian place of residence, emits tension between memory's nostalgic imagery and beauty of immediate scenery. Philosophy eventually resolves tensions by framing both the landlocked lake and the reminiscing poet as being circumstantially constrained.

2. Is your relationship to the land affected by any particular ***religious or spiritual grounding****, or does it come from a* ***specific worldview*** *of any kind?*

Poetry is my religion. I believe the universe is an unending cosmic composition designed and created by the creativity of God Almighty, not a who but a what. God is a word, and the word is Love. Thus, let us let Love be God, for God is Love. I envision heaven as a state of mind, and I am convinced that "Salvation" can be achieved through a digitally enabled compassion revolution led by the beloved of the world wielding the word as a weapon of mental mass-liberation and instrument of positive transformation.

3. What is your ***motivation and hope in writing poetry*** *related to the environment? What kind of a role do you see poetry as fulfilling?*

Poems first appeared to me spontaneously via vocabulary of scenery—mirroring sights, motions, shapes, echoing sounds, reflecting colours, reverberating rhythms, vibrations of happenings, myriad doings of living. Poems blend sights and sounds, fuse muses, motions, shapes, and colours of peoples and things. My ecologically sensitive poetry laments the unsustainability of capitalism's extreme environmental insensitivity and concurrent indecent commitment to profit over ethics. Potentially, poetry can politically mobilize a global person by a realization that words made the world what it is, so words can change the world towards working for the preservation of the bounty of Mother Earth, instead of its depletion.

"Redhill Chainsaw Massacre" memorializes protests against the construction of Hamilton's Redhill Valley Expressway and alludes implicitly to colonialism's officially muted historical ravaging of First Nations' territory and culture, literal massacres occurring in the colonial settling of Canada. Performatively, the call-and-response refrain transmits immense pain, unleashing intense emotions related to capitalism's continued desecration of natural resources.

With deep sadness we must report that Klyde Broox died in January 2024, just after recording much of his dub-poetry as now collected in a forthcoming volume with Wolsak and Wynn. Klyde was much loved and deeply respected in the Hamilton area, particularly for his work with the Afro-Canadian Caribbean Association's Black Youth program. At a celebration of life dubbed "Klyde's OutroDUBtion," his daughter Toya Brooks said, "He really believed that words can change the world, and how people communicate and treat other people in their communication can really create the future." The biographical note below is as Klyde wrote it.

Hamilton-based, Jamaican-born international dubpoet, **Klyde Broox**, a.k.a. Clyde Durm I Brooks, blends ancient oral traditions with recent digital scribal innovations; performs poetry as public art, and invites audiences to experience it as social communion. He migrated with his family to Burlington, Canada, in 1993, moved to Hamilton in 1997, started PoeMagic, and, in 2005, became the first writer of colour to win the City of Hamilton Arts Award for Literature. Broox has delivered performances, workshops and guest lectures in Jamaica, Canada, the United States, and England. He has published *PoemStorm* (Swansea, Wales, 1989) and *My Best Friend is White* (McGilligan Books, Toronto, 2005).

Linzey Corridon

1. How would you describe your ***relationship to the land****, and how long have you called a particular physical place 'home'?*

I have a strained relationship to land. A shifting relationship. I'm a Caribbean boy from Saint Vincent—a "boy of the soil," and I carry with me traces of what could have been if I'd stayed there. But I was uprooted from the Archipelago as a teenager, before I was fully formed, and now I am trying to complete that labor of formation in N. America. My mum is a Douglaa woman of African and South Asian descent and my father is of European origins, so I'm always trying to think further about how I could connect with these three regions while remaining tethered to the island [of Saint Vincent]. The principle of reciprocity drives me to try and sustain these connections, giving back to three different regions and lands that remain somewhat embedded in me.

I'm still trying to find my place in Canada: I moved to Montreal for my D.E.C. studies, and then I completed an undergrad and M.A. Politics remains at the beating heart of Quebec's autonom—here's a constant tension between radicals and xenophobic ultra-conservatives that I found very energizing, though it can be scary to try to navigate a balance between those extremes. Living in Quebec demanded that I cultivate practices of equity as one way to remain balanced while navigating both peoples and the land. We often talk about equity and equality as existing exclusively between *homo sapiens*, but then we completely refuse to acknowledge how the lands on which we settle should be treated in a similar fashion. I finally left Quebec for Ontario, to do a PhD at McMaster—so now, how to negotiate the different tensions in Hamilton? At one point I'm moving through a smog-filled industrial landscape, and at another I'm up at Albion Falls: how do I make sense of the schism between these two worlds? I think home is where we make it, so I'm content with contemplating where I'm at, physically and psychically, now that I'm transplanted elsewhere once more.

2. Is your relationship to the land affected by any particular ***religious or spiritual grounding****, or does it come from a* ***specific worldview*** *of any kind?*

I'm fascinated by finding overlaps between two or more extremes—learning to live in a place where we don't have to choose, for instance, between embracing religion on the one side and admonishing religion on the other. I've spent a lot of time thinking about what it means to be religious outside of the particular context that I was raised in, which was largely Catholic and Adventist. On the island Christianity is a colonial, imperial vacuum, a very severe kind of religion with no room for non-Christians to thrive. But my grandmother's people came to Trinidad as indentured labourers, and they remain strongly rooted in the Hinduism they brought with them. I recall also having access to my village's Shango Baptist community as a child. So, particularly as a reader and an academic, it has been difficult for me not to pay attention to all of the other life that was happening outside of the Christian world. Since moving to Canada I've given a lot of time to thinking about Indigenous world views, about what the custodians of Turtle Island have believed and how they have lived, and how they've continued to transform those principles.

I'm really interested as a human being in stepping back and not jumping to conclusions without having first observed what is taking place before me. I'm interested in how I remain connected to the mini-worlds of other beings, to the human as well as the extra-human. I think a lot about equity, rather than feeding into contemporary popular discourses on equality. Nature isn't a place of equality because there are always visible and nonvisible hierarchies at play, but we can learn from those hard truths which we observe in nature, the way trees have learned to share with one another, and animals have learned to allow space to kin and non-kin. If we set up equality as the goal of the human species, then we set ourselves up to inevitably fail, but if as a human collective we consider the promises of equity, we can begin to work towards an altruistic culture of reciprocity. We give what we must to those who justly require our support. We receive graciously from other beings when we are in need of aid. Perhaps my adherence to principles of equity amount to a kind of religion, who knows? What I do believe with certainty is that we can contribute to a collective environmental ethic by listening to the world around us, even when we're just sitting on a deck, drinking tea and acknowledging the raccoon next door—we don't have to go to the extreme of living on a ranch and raising organic vegetables and making our own honey!

*3. What is your **motivation and hope in writing poetry** related to the environment? What kind of a role do you see poetry as fulfilling?*

I want readers to feel that they can be in relation to the world around them. Panic about the environment and climate change can be paralyzing; I would like for my poems to encourage hope, and for my practice to demand that humans as a species begin to imagine otherwise. The Cree poet and public intellectual Billy-Ray Belcourt said recently that he wishes he could just "be the poem," and not the writer. I, too, would love to be the poem first, not the poet. My wish is for readers to desire a similar mode of being, to embody that thing of beauty, without the signs of hardship and labour that it took to create it.

Linzey Corridon is a Vanier Scholar, an educator, and a PhD student in the Department of English and Cultural Studies at McMaster University. Born and raised in St. Vincent and the Grenadines, he is an islander of Afro-Caribbean, Indo-Caribbean, and European descent. A settler who first moved to Tiotià:ke / Montreal, he now resides in Ohròn:wakon / Hamilton. Having lived in two vastly different geopolitical sites of the Americas, Linzey is interested in exploring how one's relationship to the land shifts depending on one's physical & psychic locations. As a recent newcomer to Ohròn:wakon, he is learning to live in relation to the environment and all its complexities.

Corri Daniels

1. How would you describe your ***relationship to the land****, and how long have you called a particular physical place 'home'?*

I come from many different places. I come from George Gordon First Nation in Saskatchewan, home of my birth family. I was born and raised in Calgary, and I've lived in southwestern Ontario for thirty years. Living in this area was the closest to home that I have ever felt. There are so many beautiful spots.

My husband and I have moved to Temagami to run a cottage resort on the lake. It's a world of ancient forests that have been there forever, and it feels sacred to stand under these trees. So, when you ask, "what's your relationship?" what I'm feeling is humbleness on the land. It's not one specific place, but how you are connected when you're on the land.

2. Is your relationship to the land affected by any particular ***religious or spiritual grounding****, or does it come from a* ***specific worldview*** *of any kind?*

I've been lucky enough to receive various teachings from Indigenous elders. In these teachings, the earth is our relative; we have to treat it with the utmost respect. For example, we have full moon ceremonies where we honour the moon as our grandmother. The sun is considered our grandfather, who comes up every day and gives us warmth and light. We honour every step we take; it's a very gentle walk that we must take on our mother earth.

I feel spiritually grounded when I'm outside of the city, and on the land. That medicine has helped me on my own healing journey as a Sixties Scoop survivor who grew up in a middle-class home, not knowing who I was until

I turned forty. There's been a lot of transformation as far as my perspectives on religion in itself. Being on the land is more of a spiritual experience than religious to me.

*3. What is your **motivation and hope in writing poetry** related to the environment? What kind of a role do you see poetry as fulfilling?*

Poetry evokes emotion and brings out your senses. When I write poems, I'm trying to make people feel something they normally wouldn't feel. Poetry evokes emotion naturally.

In "Forest Songs," I wanted to show how the tree has its own spirit. I wanted the flow of the poem to imitate the sound of trees moving in the wind. Trees have their own relationships, and in our culture, they hold wisdom, history, stories, and timelines. When a brisk wind is coming through, and those trees are communicating, it's hypnotizing. I stop everything and listen. When I see a birch tree at the end of its thirty-year life, I put tobacco down and say a prayer, thanking it for being there during that time—giving shelter and shade, providing a home for birds and critters, providing space on the rivers. [In this poem,] I wanted to pay homage back with something meaningful. To give it life.

Corri Daniels–*Osawa Waskipitew Piyisis Iskew*—is a Cree 'Sixties Scoop' survivor from George Gordon First Nation in Treaty 4 territory, Saskatchewan. Corri is a published writer and poet, chosen to participate with the Audible.ca 2021 Indigenous Writers Circle. She was longlisted for the 2017 CBC Short Story prize for her short story "Sweet Grass Spirits," and was published in the *Chapter House Journal* for her poem "Forest Songs." She was chosen for the Emerging Indigenous Writers Reading Series in Toronto in 2018, and was shortlisted for the 2020 Indigenous Voices Awards. Having spent 30 years in SW Ontario, Corri lives in Northern Ontario with her husband Peter, Bernedoodle Piper and their "old lady" poodle, Pringle.

Brian Day

1. How would you describe your ***relationship to the land****, and how long have you called a particular physical place 'home'?*

I'm a recent transplant from Ontario to British Columbia. I grew up in BC, but lived almost my entire adult life in Toronto. In Toronto I had a sporadic, intermittent, and partial relationship to land, because I felt very much confined to an urban environment. There were occasional excursions out to natural spaces, but these would usually include a couple of hours in traffic on each end. One of the things I noted, when I would go out on a day trip, or to Loyola House in Guelph for a weekend retreat, was that when I came to a natural space, I was not available to it; there was no sense of access or permeability. I felt foreign to the land, to nature, and was keenly aware of that. It would usually take a few days—when I had a few days, which was not very often—for that loosening to take place. I've lived on Salt Spring Island for two and a half years now, and this is the first time that I have lived in a continuous relationship with land.

2. Is your relationship to the land affected by any particular ***religious or spiritual grounding****, or does it come from a* ***specific worldview*** *of any kind?*

There are a lot of elements to this. I grew up with a Christian background, so certainly one of the elements at play in my interaction with nature is my seeking—or listening for—the holy as I've encountered it in the Christian tradition. I'm also very much aware of a certain insufficiency in the tradition's view of nature, so it's not simply that I am extending something from my Christian background, but that nature is teaching me something which, in some way, supplements or supersedes what I have known.

I read *The Universe Story* by Thomas Berry and Brian Swimme some years ago, and this shifted my religious focus from more text- and tradition-oriented to more Earth-oriented, not only in regard to creation, but also in the diachronic sense, of the history and development of the natural world and the universe. This is something I've been yearning toward for some time, but which I'm not yet fully able to articulate: a sort of universe religion, a sense of the divine moving in and through what we know scientifically as the long creation of the universe, life, and human creativity.

As I've thought and written more about the process of the universe and creation, there's been some shifting or loosening of my God concept. When I started it was more creator-focused, but now there are three elements: God as creator, God as creation, God as creativity. Sometimes it's unsettling to live with those three, but it feels also that there is considerable richness in the shifts and shadings between them.

3. What is your ***motivation and hope in writing poetry*** *related to the environment? What kind of a role do you see poetry as fulfilling?*

When I was on a retreat on spirituality and ecology in Guelph, we were shown a clip of a video by Joanna Macy. In it, she was talking about the work that needs to be done to address climate change. In addition to the practical actions to stop what we're doing wrong and to start acting more responsibly and respectfully, she talked about the cultural work that needs to be done, to reorient us toward the cultural framework and ideas that we need to live in right relationship with the Earth. That was of great consolation to me! Because I had always felt myself to be rather useless in doing any sort of practical work in relation to the Earth crisis. But it immediately made sense to me that we not only need action in government policies and technologies—we also need cultural change.

I hope that poetry, literature, and the arts more broadly might have a role in helping us to both imagine and move toward the world we want—one that's more about community with other human and nonhuman beings, that helps us to restore our relations with the Earth, and that reconfigures our relations with the divine. One of the roles of poetry is presenting—harshly, frankly, even alarmingly—where we are and where we could be if we keep living the way we are now. But poetry should also imagine turnings before we reach disaster, and alternatives to disaster. It should provide some vision of the whole world—the natural and human and religious world—that we aspire to live in.

Brian Day grew up in British Columbia's Fraser Valley, lived most of his adult life in Toronto, where he taught elementary school, and now lives on BC's Salt Spring Island. He has published four books of poetry with Guernica Editions, including *The Daring of Paradise* and *Conjuring Jesus*. *The Making*, a book-length poem retelling the universe through science and story, was published by Wipf and Stock in February 2024. On Salt Spring he writes, reads, tells stories, swims, gardens, and walks by the sea.

Adam Dickinson

1. How would you describe your ***relationship to the land****, and how long have you called a particular physical place 'home'?*

I would describe my relationship to the land as metabolic. I'm interested in thinking about the way in which I'm not just in the land, but the land is in me. I'm embedded in all kinds of flows—linguistic, cultural, chemical and nutrient. I grew up in Bracebridge, Ontario, on the landscape of the Canadian Shield, and I think about my historical connections to that place, about the flows of energy—petrochemicals, industry, capital—but also how history and memory accumulate as a kind of energetic flow. I'm half Ukrainian and half British, so I think about that mash-up of histories and cultures, of extreme eastern Europe and extreme western Europe.

I also think about metabolism in relation to where I live now, in Niagara, in southern Ontario, which is itself the cradle of industrial Canada, and which bears the marks of that history through its metabolic flows, whether it is the eutrophication of Lake Erie, or PCBs in various watercourses. When I did work for my book *Anatomic*, I discovered PCBs inside my blood and my fat, and I thought about my relationship to land in a different way, as I bear these traces. Place is no longer just about where you live, but about the way in which a body absorbs its environment, becomes written over by its environment, and passes that environment down through generations. The body is a trans-local place, a kind of mobile bioregion. We write the environment by altering landscapes and ecosystems, but the environment writes us too, sometimes as a function of our having changed it. We have to think carefully about the kinds of energy sources we want to use as we transition away from fossil fuels because the products of those decisions will get inside us.

I'm interested in the accumulation and dissipation of metabolic rifts, and in making those visible. Dietitians, economists, and environmentalists all encounter metabolic rifts: the Anthropocene is a long history of rifts of all kinds, even in social relations, in the circulation of capital and uneven distributions of wealth. Therefore, my home is not just physical, but it is also temporal and historically located: home is a very complex intersection of vertical and horizontal axes. In a physical sense I'll always be attached to where I grew up, but as I grow older, my sense of my home and my place and my community has expanded: that reinforces how the local necessarily involves global influence.

2. Is your relationship to the land affected by any particular ***religious or spiritual grounding****, or does it come from a* ***specific worldview*** *of any kind?*

I understand my relationship to home and place the way that I imagine monarch butterflies understand their migration routes—that's to say, it feels right to go this way, in the absence of any other explanation. My relationship with land and home is scalar and harmonic: I feel the resonance between different levels and times. That relationship is aesthetic, and it's spiritual as well, but it's also scientific: these words merge together for me through the word "wondrous." Wonder is perhaps a way of stepping around "the sublime," or other religiously inflected terms.

3. What is your ***motivation and hope in writing poetry*** *related to the environment? What kind of a role do you see poetry as fulfilling?*

My books have increasingly involved intersections between poetry and science: I'm interested in using the procedures and experimental protocols of science as a way of reimagining poetic forms and poetic inquiry. Poems themselves are little experimental processes; they sometimes even begin with hypotheses that they prove or disprove, or explode in some way. Poetry is well-positioned to grapple with some of the epistemological and conceptual difficulties that we face right now because of its engagement with the limits of language. We're being forced now to consider the limits of thinking, as we try to reimagine what it means to understand community, society, and our relationship to the environment. One way of thinking about the role of poetry is that it aims to reenergize our relationship with these communities of language. Poetry makes the illegible legible; what I'm interested in doing is making metabolic writing, social and biological writing, visible so we can talk about it.

I am interested in writing that shifts conventional frames of signification. At some level, there is hope in this because new possibilities emerge—an experiment itself (in both art and science) is ultimately a hopeful enterprise. When we start shifting and broadening frames of signification, we invite otherwise marginal elements to signify and we can expand our sense of what matters. That is also an ethical move: who or what signifies? This is an endless well of creativity in both science and art.

Adam Dickinson is the author of four books of poetry, including *Anatomic* (Coach House Books), a finalist for the Raymond Souster Award, and winner of the Alanna Bondar Memorial Book Prize from the Association for Literature, Environment, and Culture in Canada. His work has been nominated for the Governor General's Award for Poetry, and twice for the Trillium Book Award for Poetry. He was also a finalist for the Canadian Broadcasting Corporation (CBC) Poetry Prize and the K.M. Hunter Artist Award in Literature. He was selected, along with Claudia Rankine (USA) and Valzhyna Mort (Belarus), to be a member of the jury for the 2022 Griffin Poetry Prize. He teaches English and Creative Writing at Brock University in St. Catharines, Ontario.

Joanne Epp

1. How would you describe your ***relationship to the land****, and how long have you called a particular physical place 'home'?*

I grew up in a really small Saskatchewan town, and so I was always in a place where I was conscious of the surrounding countryside. I was always interested in the little things, like the stones on our driveway, or the snail-shells in the slough behind our house, or butterflies and birds and flower blossoms—as I still am! I think I always saw the land as a place to belong to, a place to be from, a place to enjoy. I'd also say now that the land is something to be respected and loved and cared for. I moved to Ontario with my husband when I was about 28, first to Ottawa for six years, and then Toronto for three. Toronto was nice in its way, but I always felt there was a bit too much of it. Now we've been in Winnipeg for more than 20 years, and it's been important to intentionally get to know Winnipeg as a place, as land. What I've been finding is that the more you get to know a place—like the creek in my area of the city, and the small lake in Whiteshell Provincial Park that my family often visits—the more you can see in it: you never quite see everything. When I visit the Hamilton area, I connect there too, because my brother, who lives in Dundas, has taken a lot of trouble to get to know the area where he lives, and he always takes me on walks in the Dundas valley or on a hike to some other beautiful place, like Hilton Falls.

2. Is your relationship to the land affected by any particular ***religious or spiritual grounding****, or does it come from a* ***specific worldview*** *of any kind?*

Definitely from a Christian grounding. I was taught in Sunday School from age three that God created the world—but since then it's been a slow process learning what it means to respect the world as God's creation, to see the whole world as holy ground—starting with something as simple as not littering. At Bible college I learned about the symbolism and overarching themes in the creation accounts in Genesis, how they portray a world that is created good and as a home for us. Even the forces of chaos are created things under God's umbrella. More recently, one thing that stood out to me from a sermon was that the non-human creation has its own relationship to God, apart from humans—which can be seen in many places in scripture, not just in Genesis. I've become very conscious that I don't own the land, but I do belong to it. The ecological theologian Norman Wirzba says the biblical view of creation is not primarily about the origin of the world but about a relationship. And in my poetry I'm gradually finding words to articulate that.

*3. What is your **motivation and hope in writing poetry** related to the environment? What kind of a role do you see poetry as fulfilling?*

My writing has been more and more about the natural world over the past 20 years. In 2008 I went on a writing retreat in Saskatchewan in mid-May, when nature was just exploding with new life, and there were a lot of birds migrating through. I did a lot of walking, and spent at least as much time observing the natural world as I did writing, and that got something started. I began to see my job as a poet as being attentive to the world, and what I write as growing out of love for the world. I can't write political poetry, but what does work for me is writing out of a feeling of connection and attraction. Like Jane Siberry says of her song-writing, I write about whatever captivates me, and I try to capture it back, so the reader can also be captivated.

Joanne Epp lives in Winnipeg, but has connections to southern Ontario through her brother, who has lived there for many years, and who has made a concerted effort to get to know the area. She writes: "Whenever I visit, whether alone or with my family, there's always an excursion involved: a walk to one of the many waterfalls around Dundas, or a drive to a conservation area." Joanne's second full-length poetry collection, *Cattail Skyline*, was published by Turnstone Press in 2021. She is co-translator, with Sally Ito and Sarah Klassen, of *Wonder-Work: Selected Sonnets of Catharina Regina von Greiffenberg* (CMU Press, 2023). When not writing, she may be found practicing the organ, making linocut prints, or photographing wildflowers by the creek. Website: joanneepp.com

Jaidyn Fenton

1. How would you describe your ***relationship to the land****, and how long have you called a particular physical place 'home'?*

I'd describe my relationship to the land as very intimate; farmland has always been something I've aspired to live on. In fact, my ancestors in Jamaica took care of much tillage; my aunt owns a bed-and-breakfast, a smallholding with animals, and she works the fields nearly every day. I've adopted my family's experience there as my own, and feel very connected to it. Growing up in Canada, I have visited farms for fun and still value that experience. I've lived in various cities, namely Hamilton, ON for eleven years, and now Montreal, QC. There was a lot of forestry and trails where I used to live in Hamilton. In this anthology, my poem has been created in concordance with a painting at the Art Gallery of Hamilton; it is a picture of Amherst Island. I wrote about a farm there, and that land is quite like acreage around Hamilton.

2. Is your relationship to the land affected by any particular ***religious or spiritual grounding****, or does it come from a* ***specific worldview*** *of any kind?*

My relationship to the land is tied to my worldview of seeing it as a valuable creation of God. I believe that we should be taking care of God's nature, never polluting it, but preserving its beauty.

3. What is your ***motivation and hope in writing poetry*** *related to the environment? What kind of a role do you see poetry as fulfilling?*

I want people to get an insight into the delight of the outdoors. I see poetry as fulfilling the role of showing a pristine perspective of life on the farm, in contrast to the stigma that people have towards rural areas. A lot of people see farming as tedious, but I wanted to present it as something fun. My goal was to display several different settings and perspectives on farming, from a hard day's work to the peace that can be achieved far from city life. I want anyone who reads my poem to feel like they too are experiencing an adventure. It's meant to be a passionate piece.

Jaidyn Fenton is a 20-year-old spoken word poet, artist, and lover of nature. Born in Barrie, Ontario, and currently living in Dorval, Quebec, Jaidyn is all too familiar with a change of scenery and the great outdoors. Her experience with the rural life and passion for landscape is evident in her poem "Amherst Island." She has been interviewed for and featured in both *The Hamilton Spectator* and the *Toronto Caribbean Newspaper*. Jaidyn is well-known for her performances and poetic highlights at One Mic Educators and The Hamilton Youth Poets. She can be found on Instagram (@jaidynfenton) and can be contacted at jaidynfentonbfa@gmail.com.

Linda Frank

1. How would you describe your ***relationship to the land****, and how long have you called a particular physical place 'home'?*

The most impressionable part of my life took place in Montreal where I grew up. It had a huge effect upon me. My father bought a house there, which was the only land he ever owned. In those days, my mother opened the door, said "Bye!" and I'd get on my bike to roam around. We were left at such a young age to discover the world around us, so we explored orchards and forests and anything else we could find.

One of the reasons I was happy to move to Hamilton from Montreal in the late '70s was how easy it is here to get into nature, whether that meant the Rail Trail or Cootes Paradise, and for sure being so close to Lake Ontario, and an easy drive to Lake Erie—and, of course, Lake Huron. I also had no idea before I moved here how different it would be, living close to an area where you can grow peaches: we had five peach trees in Hamilton when we bought our house.

We also have this amazing property in Southampton, right on Lake Huron. Of course, we're conscious of the fact that there is a reserve two miles north of us, the Saugeen First Nation, and one to the east of us, and we're sitting in this little pocket between them both. We're so aware of whose land this is, our incredible privilege, and all that it means.

On top of this, I have a huge relationship to the water. One of the things about being so near to the Great Lakes is that I get to experience the vastness. If you sit on my deck up in Southampton, you would think you're sitting next to the ocean. The weather just comes at you across the lake. The sky, the waves, they all hit you out here. You get to sit in this immensity, and the little things—caterpillars, insects—pop out, juxtaposed in and against this huge system we live in.

Although I'm not necessarily connected to the land, I'd consider myself connected to everything that's on the land. I've always been interested in the little creatures—insects in particular—and I can sit out here, watching the hummingbirds zoom around, close enough to touch. And that's a privilege for sure.

2. Is your relationship to the land affected by any particular ***religious or spiritual grounding****, or does it come from a* ***specific worldview*** *of any kind?*

I never grew up with a particular practice of religion. I'm Jewish, and I grew up aware of that, but it was more of a cultural knowledge. I knew about my ancestors, who wandered a lot, because Jews were displaced from their homes and tended to have jobs which they could take with them wherever they went. As an Anglo growing up in Quebec, I was very aware of being English in a French province. There were some parallels that I felt: the Jews losing their country, just as the Quebecois were losing their language and feeling like they were losing their country. My worldview is really a political sense: I'm more aware of what it means to lose your country or your language than of what it is to be part of those things.

3. What is your ***motivation and hope in writing poetry*** *related to the environment? What kind of a role do you see poetry as fulfilling?*

Who knows? Do poets ever know what they're doing with their writing?

My motivation isn't to convince anyone of anything, but I want people to think critically, to evaluate their relationship to the environment. It's been so rewarding to hear my readers respond to my work and share the ways it has made them rethink how they treat the living world.

Linda Frank was born in Montreal and now lives in Hamilton, Ontario. A retired professor from Mohawk College, she has written three books of poetry: *Cobalt Moon Embrace, Insomnie Blues*, and *Kahlo: The World Split Open*, which was shortlisted for the Pat Lowther Award. She is a past winner of the Banff Centre's Bliss Carman Poetry Award and has been shortlisted for the National Magazine Awards.

Marilyn Gear Pilling

1. How would you describe your ***relationship to the land****, and how long have you called a particular physical place 'home'?*

Several years ago, I was lucky enough to travel to Newfoundland with three other poets to study with Canadian poet Don McKay. He read my work and identified me as a phenomenologist. I must have looked at him blankly, because he went on to say that I should read the book *The Spell of the Sensuous* by David Abram, and that would explain it all. In that book I found a perfect description of what my relationship to the land is: "Whenever I quiet the persistent chatter of words within my head, I find … this improvised duet between my animal body and the fluid, breathing landscape that it inhabits."

I have called a particular place home since I was a young child. I grew up in Waterloo, and have lived in Hamilton for all of my married life. But my home is in Huron County, specifically the East Wawanosh area, more specifically the farm. For me, it's the field of the deeply familiar: I call it "the field next to love." Along what was then the Sixth Line lived most of my mother's kin. My father also had a farm there. Although we lived in Waterloo, we made the two-hour journey every Friday night and returned home on Sunday night. We also lived on the farm every summer and holiday.

For some writers, you find that there is something in the life that becomes a well for the writing, that supplies the blood for the writing and that creates a pervasive theme that runs through the *oeuvre* like a river. Most of my work is inspired by "the field next to love." All of the generations before me are now gone from this earth, but they are alive in my heart and mind; they've migrated from the outer world to my inner world. "The field next to love" has become a major metaphor that occupies a central place in my inner landscape, and no matter what subject I'm writing about, the farm feeds it.

2. Is your relationship to the land affected by any particular ***religious or spiritual grounding****, or does it come from a* ***specific worldview*** *of any kind?*

I was raised in the Judeo-Christian tradition and went to church until I started university at age seventeen. In Sunday school and church we studied the King James Version of the Bible: I think that I might not have become a writer without it. We memorized many passages from the Bible, and I absorbed not so much the message and the content but rather the words as they created a kind of music in my ears.

My worldview now is to respect and marvel at the natural world, to drink in through my senses the natural world and the other creatures who inhabit it, and to write about it. An activity that stems from my worldview is that I pick up garbage. I feel the litter of food containers and other garbage to be a desecration of the environment, and I use the word "desecrate" rather than, say, "pollute" because it means to violate a sacred place or thing.

3. What is your ***motivation and hope in writing poetry*** *related to the environment? What kind of a role do you see poetry as fulfilling?*

Well, I could say, as Auden did, that "poetry makes nothing happen," or I could say what I used to tell my adult students, "poetry is the way to the water of life," or I could say something in between, such as—a poem is sometimes able to ignite a fire in a human being, who might then go on, for instance, to lead a campaign against killing rhinoceros for their horns. (The rhinoceros has existed for fifty million years. We have existed for one fifth of one million years.) Good poetry has a quiet way of opening a reader's heart and mind to the incredible world of nature that surrounds us, and that can only be a good thing.

Marilyn Gear Pilling lives in Hamilton, Ontario. She is the author of three collections of short fiction, the most recent of which is *On Huron's Shore* (Demeter Press), five collections of poetry, one chapbook, *Estrangement* (The Alfred Gustav Press, 2017), and is the editor of a book of poetry, *Evenings on Paisley Avenue*. She has won, and/or placed, in forty-five national contests for poetry, literary non-fiction and fiction, including the CBC literary awards, the Western Magazine Awards and *Descant's* first place award for Best Canadian Poem. She has, as well, won twenty local Hamilton awards in those three genres. Pilling's work has been broadcast on the CBC and she has read in many venues, including Eden Mills, Harbourfront, the Banff Centre in Alberta, the historic Shakespeare and Company bookstore in Paris, France, and in Holguin, Cuba. Several of her poems have been translated into Spanish. Pilling participated in the 2013 CBC poetry contest as a winnowing judge. She is past President of the Hamilton Poetry Centre.

Alyssa General

1. How would you describe your ***relationship to the land****, and how long have you called a particular physical place 'home'?*

Alyssa niwakhsennò:ten, Kanyen'kehá:ka niwakonhwentsyò:ten, wakenyáhton. I wanted to introduce myself in my native language first.

Our connection to the land, here, is a new thing in a sense. After the war of 1812, when the Mohawks had sided with the English, we ended up within this community of Six Nations, the Haldimand tract. I've known this as my home for the longest time, but also recognize that our traditional territory, *Kanatsyoharé:ke*, is my home place as well. Whenever we talk about who we are, introducing ourselves in our language, we always talk about being from the home community we had back in our traditional territory, in the Adirondack mountains and placed within the Mohawk valley. We talk about being *Kanyen'kehá:ka*, or "person of the flint." The relationship is not as much about flint as it is about chert, which becomes Herkimer diamonds that are unique to a certain section in the Adirondack mountains

2. Is your relationship to the land affected by any particular ***religious or spiritual grounding****, or does it come from a* ***specific worldview*** *of any kind?*

I would say it's all of them. I wouldn't even call it a religion, really. Our way of being is so intrinsically tied to the land. Kanyen'kéha, Mohawk, is a verb-based language. It's polysynthetic, so every word we have is pretty much a sentence. It's descriptive in the way it relates to you; you always have a relationship with whatever you're talking about, even if it's a chair, a table, or something out in nature. A great example of this is *Yethi'nisténha Ohwentsya* which is "our mother the earth." It comes back to our stewardship over the land and how we are birthed with the responsibility to take care of this person that takes care of us.

When we give thanks in our thanksgiving address, *'Ohén:ton Karihwatéhkwen*, meaning "the matter is before all else," we thank everything in creation that helps keep us alive. We're sort of at the bottom of the chain, even though in more modern times we consider ourselves to be the top dog in the world. We don't realize how much we rely on creation to sustain us. This speech is one of the most important speeches; we do it before we conduct meetings, before we start our day, before any huge matter comes to pass; we give thanks to all of these things within creation that help us live.

Being given that sense of responsibility really does change the way you appreciate the land that you come from. I may not have always thought this way. We grew up in a forest--my father was an artist, and my mother was a homemaker, so we had these really good experiences of nature. But there's this phenomenon in language-learning called the Sapir-Whorf hypothesis: when you're learning a language, it changes the way that you think. That's so true for our languages. Language revitalization is crucial to the health of not only our lands, but also our people. It's as if the health of one is tied to the health of another, because once you start learning the language, you start to see this interwoven-ness—how our language is tied to the place we come from, to the land, to creation sustaining us.

3. What is your ***motivation and hope in writing poetry*** *related to the environment? What kind of a role do you see poetry as fulfilling?*

I wasn't sure I was going to write poetry for this piece, at first. I'm an artist, a linguist, and a teacher first, so poetry is sort of my own catharsis. I'm very into language. I love words, and combinations of words that articulate the relationships the way I feel them. Sometimes it's such a hard process to come by—to write something that really speaks to the mixture of emotions that you feel. The cathartic part is the articulating. How do I articulate all of this emotion in a way that helps somebody glean a sense of empathy from it?

This poem in particular came from a mixture of love, anger, and healing. I actually think I wrote it for my grandchildren, but also for anybody who is furthering their relationship with their land, recognizing that there's such strength in the land, as a reminder not to pave over that beauty.

Alyssa M. General is Mohawk Nation Turtle Clan from Six Nations of the Grand River Territory. She is an artist, educator, and language revitalist. She has helped create a series of films in Kanyen'kéha with Onkwawén:na Kentyóhkwa, has developed illustrations for the children's television show *Tóta tánon Ohkwá:ri*, and has received national recognition for her poem "Enkonte'nikonhrakwaríhsya'te." Alyssa has worked as an artist-educator with the Royal Conservatory of Music, a graphic designer with the Six Nations Language Commission and the Kawenní:io Language Preservation Project, as well as with Wahta Mohawks, and she is the artistic director with the publishing company Spirit & Intent.

Catherine Graham

1. How would you describe your ***relationship to the land****, and how long have you called a particular physical place 'home'?*

I was born in Hamilton but grew up in Grimsby in a house that backed onto the Niagara Escarpment. I live in Toronto now and whenever I drive back that way, I feel a pull to that landscape. In addition to a water-filled limestone quarry we later lived beside, these formative places from my past continue to serve my imagination and feed my poetic process. I still think of them both as 'home.'

2. Is your relationship to the land affected by any particular ***religious or spiritual grounding****, or does it come from a* ***specific worldview*** *of any kind?*

My relationship to the land grounds me emotionally, physically and spiritually. Places where I once lived—the Niagara Escarpment or the water-filled limestone quarry mentioned above—continue to spark my imagination as a writer. Walking through city parks here in Toronto or at the cottage in Haliburton also connects me to the land and reminds me that we are all part of nature, there is no separation.

My parents both died during my undergraduate years and I connect with them through walking the land and encountering creatures that live there. For example, deer, my father; the Northern cardinal, my mother. A few years ago, while walking to and from Princess Margaret Hospital for radiation treatment from our home in Queen West, Toronto, I began connecting to feathers on city sidewalks. I was diagnosed with the disease the exact age my mother died from it and she became my spirit mentor during this unsettling time. Feathers fallen from birds became my sign she was with me. Nature speaks to us in many ways; we just have to listen.

3. What is your ***motivation and hope in writing poetry*** *related to the environment? What kind of a role do you see poetry as fulfilling?*

I was one of many editors for the anthology *Watch Your Head: Writers & Artists Respond to the Climate Crisis*, spearheaded by Kathryn Mockler. It's a collection of poems, stories, essays, and artwork that "sound the alarm on the present and future consequences of the climate emergency." I see this work as a place of hope as well as a call to climate-justice action. All proceeds are donated to RAVEN and Climate Justice Toronto. There's a website too.

There's tension and complexity in art, particularly poetry. It embraces ambiguity, and its imagery can make readers 'see' different things at the same time. Seeing leads to empathy, and empathy leads to care, to action. Learning to 'see' what is there in our environment—before it's too late—can be a step towards creating change.

Catherine Graham is a poet, novelist, podcast host, and creative writing instructor based in Toronto. *Æther: An Out-of-Body Lyric* was a finalist for the Trillium Book Award, Toronto Book Award, and won the Fred Kerner Book Award. She leads the Toronto International Festival of Authors' Book Club and co-hosts the Hummingbird Podcast—part of the WNED PBS Amplify app. *Put Flowers Around Us and Pretend We're Dead: New and Selected Poems* is her latest book. www.catherinegraham.com @catgrahampoet

David Haskins (1944-2023)

1. How would you describe your ***relationship to the land****, and how long have you called a particular physical place 'home'?*

I've lived in Grimsby since 1989, so I guess I could call this place home. Before that, though, my wife and I lived on the edge of the lake, on top of a cliff that used to erode into the lake bit by bit each year. I think I had a bit of nervous angst about that because I don't swim: I like to be on the water, but I'm not crazy about being in it. Before that, when I was going to high-school and university, I lived in the town of Beamsville. And I've always lived in this general area, in this geographical floodplain. Initially I had a great deal of trouble relating to the place I found myself in, because it wasn't anything like the place I came from as an eight-year-old child: a typical response of any immigrant. I came from England, a self-contained island with an established social hierarchy: no wilderness to speak of—it's all managed. When you arrive in Canada by boat, you sail down the St Lawrence to the middle of this huge country, to the Great Lakes—you don't get time to figure it out. Nothing seemed to fit: I couldn't do anything my peers at school could do, and I tried to get rid of my accent as soon as I could. My father's family business in England had been a nursery: he was a grower, so I was always conscious of growing things. But he couldn't start a nursery of his own here because his horticulture certification wasn't complete. So he worked as a labourer at several nurseries; that stuff was very much part of my upbringing. I did also have a passion for butterflies, and I used to spend hours chasing them, and bring them home to collect in a butterfly case—much more colourful and much bigger than English butterflies.

2. Is your relationship to the land affected by any particular ***religious or spiritual grounding****, or does it come from a* ***specific worldview*** *of any kind?*

The short answer would be No. I was brought up in the Anglican church; my father was a lay reader and he led the choir. Because I was in the choir, I never went to Sunday School or got caught up on the biblical stories. I did everything in the church, but it was all ritual: I don't feel that I got a kind of spiritual grounding. When I went to university I became more of an existentialist than anything, not least because it helped to explain the fair degree of absurdity in the world. Now I don't tend to name any particular philosophy. But in a way my immigrant experience was a kind of worldview—it certainly governed me, like baggage, much longer than I wanted it to: it gave me a kind of inferiority complex as a child. Growing up I spent a lot of time alone outside in the natural world, and so I cared about it as my world.

3. What is your ***motivation and hope in writing poetry*** *related to the environment? What kind of a role do you see poetry as fulfilling?*

As a child in England I was given Beatrix Potter and *The Wind in the Willows*: they're miniatures of British society, with the whole caste system. Canadian animal stories aren't like that: they're real, every Canadian animal dies in the jaws of another one—they're written about without being anthropomorphized. I see the writer's job as to name, not to characterize. I think I still am basically an Imagist poet: if I can use poetry for a kind of direct apprehension, I want to do that, rather than build narratives that are extensions of human invention. Insofar as there's a thread of violence in my poetry about the environment, it's because I don't think you can prevent violence happening in human interactions with the natural world.

But it's a complicated issue: the way First Nations people used to kill turtles around here, for instance, seemed very violent, even though then they used every part of the turtle. If you're a farmer you live with decay and death as a real thing—you prune out the dead so the new can come on. It's a cyclical thing—even manure is a symbol of life through death, using something that's been cast off to create new life. I could say that handing a farmer a poem is useless cull, like a damaged peach that can't be put in the basket. But the farmer I wrote about in my poem about peaches died young of cancer that they believe was caused by the sprays that he used. So in poetry I can link up a bunch of things that normally don't get juxtaposed; there's a compulsion to articulate.

I was talking with Patrick Lane about what a poem is and where it comes from and he said, You've only three places to look when you judge a poem: the groin, the heart, and the head. If it impacts any one of those three, it's a good poem; if it impacts more than one, publish it.

It was with great sadness that we learned of the death of David Haskins in April 2023. David had been a strong supporter of this anthology project, and we had very much enjoyed our interview with him in 2022. We have left his interview summary as he ratified it, and his biographical note as he wrote it. We wonder if he got to revisit that fantasy novel.

David Haskins is the author of three books: *Blood Rises* (Guernica Editions 2020), a finalist for the 2021 Hamilton Arts Literary Award for Poetry; *This House Is Condemned* (Wolsak & Wynn 2013), a literary memoir; and *Reclamation* (Borealis 1980), his first poetry book. His work appears in over 40 literary journals (*The Oxfordian, Fiddlehead, Prism, Journal of Canadian Fiction*), anthologies (*Locations of Grief* 2020, *Tamaracks: Canadian Poetry for the 21st Century* 2018), and books (*The Beauty of Being Elsewhere* 2021, *Canadian Children's Annual* 1980). He has won first prizes from the CBC, the Canadian Authors Association, the Ontario Poetry Society, and three times from Arts Hamilton. When not cruising the countryside in his 1970 blaze orange MGB, he is working in his garden, thinking about revisiting a young adult fantasy novel.

Cornelia Hoogland

1. How would you describe your ***relationship to the land****, and how long have you called a particular physical place 'home'?*

That's like asking about my relationship to air, the invisible element we breathe. Like land, we depend on it. I'm a daughter of immigrants from the Netherlands and have lived on the west coast most of my life. As a child I grew up on a farm in the Fraser Valley where my first trip was into the cow fields. I loved the cows' long tongues over the salt-licks, and the wind prickling my skin through the sweater my Mom knit. Now I live on a small piece of land on Hornby Island, where I tend a time-consuming but rewarding garden. My biggest sojourn away from the west coast was to southwestern Ontario, to teach at the University of Western Ontario. I was predisposed not to like Ontario, but in the 20 years I spent there I came to love it. I paddled the Grand River: the fireflies alone made me love that area! It's so necessary to be called back into place. Too easy to zip along the 401 highway without noticing cows grazing in the fields.

2. Is your relationship to the land affected by any particular ***religious or spiritual grounding****, or does it come from a* ***specific worldview*** *of any kind?*

My relationship to the land is geographical, practical, imaginative—and really enjoyable! I'm rereading aboriginal accounts of the creation of the world for their worldview. Or should I say ground view; the stories speak from grounded points of view. I value my historical relationship to the land: for instance, the Dutch relationship to water. A large part of the Netherlands is built on land reclaimed from the sea. I'm also learning to be a more conscientious steward. We ran out of water on our rural property this past summer; the anxiousness around climate change is profound, and echoes, in a weird way, my parents' strong sense that catastrophe could happen at any moment. Their feeling of doom, is due, I think, to Calvinist influences, as well as their experiences of Nazi soldiers banging at the door during WWII. But as we face heatwaves, forest fires, and weather extremes, being alert to catastrophe grows frighteningly appropriate.

Everything we do is spiritual in the sense that our actions stem from our beliefs. My parents' Calvinist Christian faith mandated that children be raised to praise the beautiful world that God created, but practically, they weren't aware of ecological degradation or natural balance.

I'm interested in what lies beneath. The earth is layered and complex and goes deep underground. What are we standing on? What is hidden, or under the water? John Terpstra's idea that water resists rerouting and will retrace its former path demonstrates the resiliency of the natural world that will outlive us. I'm trying to breathe more deeply these days, especially when I'm on my morning bike-ride. Recently, on three consecutive days, I experienced a newly fallen tree on the road. I thought wow, is this a message? But when I stopped to look, I realized that there were many downed trees in the forest: it's the *road* that's the incursion, not the falling trees.

3. What is your ***motivation and hope in writing poetry*** *related to the environment? What kind of a role do you see poetry as fulfilling?*

Thank goodness my university education didn't scrub the poetry out of me, but made it fiercer! I enjoy and have become dependent on the inner life that poetry nurtures. My latest book, Cosmic Bowling—from which these poems are taken—written in collaboration with my husband, Ted Goodden, contains photographs of his 64 sculptures alongside my poems, and relates the ancient cosmology of the I Ching to geographical formations. I respect the I Ching because its proportions are often broader than those of western thought: people aren't the centre of the universe, they're part of it. It makes me look carefully at the place I am. It's also more social-minded: it helps me to move beyond a narrowly personal point of view, and be less obviously anthropocentric.

My biggest hope for my poetry is that it will do what good art has always done, which is help us to reconsider, re-examine, reclaim, and feel:

for instance, poetically reclaiming the 401—such a dominant feature in the area the anthology covers—with feeling. Even the whiney No-See-Ums have a voice, if we can listen. My mother showed me the natural world, taught me to love it, and good poetry can do something similar. My mother's word for this was, Look.

Dressed in Only a Cardigan, She Picks Up Her Tracks in the Snow (Baseline), and *Cosmic Bowling* (Guernica) are **Cornelia Hoogland's** recent publications. *Trailer Park Elegy* and *Woods Wolf Girl* were finalists for Canadian national awards. Hoogland was the winner of the 2023 Colleen Thibaudeau Outstanding Achievement in Poetry Award and has been a writer-in-residence across the country. http://www.corneliahoogland.com/

Karen (Kéké) Houle

1. How would you describe your ***relationship to the land****, and how long have you called a particular physical place 'home'?*

I feel very at home on the Earth, on "the land." I sleep outside whenever I can; my lungs feel at home in the outside moving air, my feet feel at home when they are touching stones or sand or grass,; especially when my whole body is in a lake. I feel most at home, physically, emotionally and cognitively, in the bush, in the North. I grew up in northern Ontario; my dad's family are 17th century French settlers: farmers + fishers and hunters. My mum's family are late 20th century English settlers: dairy farmers in Oxford County. These relationships with land are in me. My maternal grandmother was a naturalist: she knew her farm like the back of her hand and showed me how to forage and glean and bake and pickle with what we gathered on it. My French-Canadian father was a 9-5 civil servant who at 5:10pm donned bush clothes and walked with a rifle in the fall until dusk; a fishing rod in the spring, at 4 am. Before sunrise, before work. I was often with him. He knew the bush. He showed it respect: the water, the forest and all the creatures, especially the ones we were lucky enough to eat.

We are in relations with the land, and so, with our own nature; active with the body, the hands and the feet, the mind, the fingers, the lungs, both inside and outside our dwelling. Our sense of "land" is like a gestalt, inextricable from our patterns of physical activity. For example: I crouched down this morning and gently worked an Agaricus mushroom free from the wet grass with my hands: "the land" is that gesture in that time and at that place: my crouch, my curious fingers and my eating of that mushroom.

One is always gesturing, so one is always home-building, settling in. It's important to try to know-learn a particular physical place by actively inhabiting it with your whole self as much as you can: reading widely about its natural histories and inhabitants, handling the soils through seasons, seeing what grows over a long stretch of observing, tasting the rainwater, participating in its many cycles. Settling well as an ethos: Wherever you are, no matter how briefly, try to know the land, the bush under and around you, and let it get to know you, respectfully. This is what shifts the relation from "a home" (subject-object) to "homing" (gerund, ongoing, participatory). The newest and oldest ancestors can then participate too.

In Guelph, on the Grand River Watershed, I can enact ethical variations of the agricultural and bush relationships of my kin, but also new ones such as writing poetry about the land, and walking my dog twice daily on it. Staying in right relationship with the physical and spiritual repertoire of all our relations—worms too—is the key to humans knowing who, where and what we are, and what could be. Continually becoming "at home" on the Earth is literally a moral compass.

2. Is your relationship to the land affected by any particular ***religious or spiritual grounding****, or does it come from a* ***specific worldview*** *of any kind?*

I'm a Spinozist. Spinoza saw all matter ("things") as individuals and as alive, or "powerful," by virtue of their particular repertoire of actions—what they can do and what can be done to them—and what comes from being "located" in a particular environment or situation. I suspect even as a young pious Catholic girl, I was a closet Spinozist, an animist: seeing stones and the woods and plants and tools as Jesus' ontological equals; having their own lives and thus preferences about how they are treated, where they are, what they want to be doing or being done to. My religious work was to pay attention and find out. Plants, for instance, are very much *not* animals. They are fundamentally different. Each one. Each has their own terms of being, their own powers, their own radical life-world, even while we are side-by-side or eating them. If you pay veeeerrrrry close attention with a curious and loving mind, in waking life, or in dreams, just being quiet, you might find out; they might let you know exactly what they are trying to do or trying to be, and thus exactly what your relation to them might entail. If we actively cultivate our power of sidling up to such difference rather than making it into products, or an object of pity, or theorizing it into a sterile box, we can live well *with* the world, yes, even as it is constantly shifting underfoot and overhead and within. A view of spirited aliveness in all things suggests that it is attentiveness and careful in-habitation of our shared place that brings peace and wholeness about for all, well, enmattered beings.

3. What is your ***motivation and hope in writing poetry*** *related to the environment? What kind of a role do you see poetry as fulfilling?*

The writing of poetry is an organic, holey container that you make with words—with your mind and your hands—based on curious, loving non-appropriative relationships to exactly where you are when you are gesturing with and to the *eikos*. A poem can then express (but not necessarily describe or image) the potent livingness of being-in-relationship with, say, a particular patch of grass and cloud on a particular day: the poem weaves a word basket which is also alive. Poetry, more than any other form of literature, has a sensitive and profound capacity to allow radical difference (plant-animal, past-present, grief-joy) to be in life-filled juxtaposition. And poetry is also political because, like a turbo battery, it can zap you awake, redirect you, break your habits a titch, change your course. Isn't this exactly what we have been saying for decades "has" to happen with our general relationship to the environment? Poetry, then, can be a powerful activator of exactly what is needed; it makes of us a powerful way of being attentive in the world: "poetrying" is a verb unto itself.

Karen Houle is a poet, a translator, an academic and an urban agriculture activist. She is most noted for her 2019 poetry collection *The Grand River Watershed: A Folk Ecology*, which was a shortlisted finalist in 2019 for the Governor General's Award for English-language poetry. She previously published the poetry collections *Ballast* (2000) and *During* (2005). A philosophy professor at the University of Guelph, she has written and/or edited *Hegel and Deleuze: Together Again for the First Time* (2013) with Dr. Jim Vernon, and *Toward a New Image of Thought: Responsibility, Complexity and Abortion* (2013) and *Minor Ethics: Deleuzian Variations* (2021) with Dr. Suzanne McCullagh and Dr. Casey Ford. Recently (2021) she collaborated with Helge Dascher on the translation (French to English) of a graphic novel biography of one of the greatest English-speaking Canadian poets/songwriters of all time: Leonard Cohen: *On a Wire*.

Mark Kempf

*1. How would you describe your **relationship to the land**, and how long have you called a particular physical place 'home'?*

Home is a such a broad concept—a place, of course, or a memory or activity, perhaps. I read author Elizabeth Gilbert's definition recently, that "whatever you love more than yourself is your home." In that case there are so many things that could be called home. But I grew up in Dundas, and my appreciation for and wonder at the land started very early because our house backed onto a long narrow woodland where I spent a lot of time as a kid, playing around in the river. My dad was a canoeist from forever, and he took us to the woods early and often. Nowadays most of my canoeing is in Killarney, which is mind-blowingly beautiful, and I think of Killarney as much my home as anywhere. Actually I feel just *fortunate* that I care about the land—it's not to my credit, but I feel very blessed that it's in my life.

So my relationship to the land is ongoing. For instance, I thought this past winter was a fantastic one: lots of snow that didn't melt—and one day I just needed to go stand in some snowy woods, under the tree canopy. Our home now is in Paris and we back onto the Grand River; my wife and I make a point every day of walking down to the river at least once. We want to see how it's doing, you know: we say we're visiting with the river.

*2. Is your relationship to the land affected by any particular **religious or spiritual grounding**, or does it come from a **specific worldview** of any kind?*

I do see the land as sacred. It's that simple. The Christian communities I was in when I was younger were not good stewards of the land, and they had no angle on that at all; I've moved away from that kind of religious stance now. My dad respected the land so greatly that we just had an understanding of it, and grew up knowing it was really important and you shouldn't waste stuff. I don't really think of this as a spiritual thing, though it fills the soul. But I do think First Nations' core beliefs about the land as sacred are a very honourable and clear-cut, reasonable way of looking at it.

3. What is your ***motivation and hope in writing poetry*** *related to the environment? What kind of a role do you see poetry as fulfilling?*

In general the reason I write poetry on any subject is the same: to capture a thought that I want to express, or to stretch my wings trying something new. But I have at times tried to write stuff about the land that aims to express its glory, to honour it. I'm a historian by education, so have an ongoing interest in the subject. When our kids were young, occasionally we went to the Six Nations reserve to tour around, have lunch, and just appreciate the history of the place. So when I wrote this poem about "The Paris Raceway" at the end of our land, I thought I would add the lines from the Haldimand Proclamation. I find it difficult to include a lot of historical detail in a poem, because that doesn't seem liquid enough, and I worry that a poem like this one isn't open enough for the readers to make up their own minds. But I really enjoy editing: I do work the words of the poem around and around like clay, till it has the right feel.

I have this theory that so often the struggles of man versus man have to do with land and being displaced, and I think this poem talks about displacement in a whole bunch of ways, particularly in terms of Six Nations groups being pushed out from one place to another. There's also a displacement here of man versus nature, man moving nature out, which we won't get away with for ever: I'm pretty sure nature will reclaim itself in some other form. In this poem, what's interesting about the river is that, even though it's controlled somewhat by man and by dams upstream, it more or less has its own mind. It does whatever it's going to do: I can't go out there and control the sound of the water, you know? And the poem suggests that there can be one history that's being remembered more than another; lots of layers of competing story build up by the river.

Mark Kempf is a poet from Paris, Ontario who enjoys life along the Grand River with his wife of over forty years, and great neighbours that include a half-dozen deer plus a few beaver, osprey and eagles. He spends as much time as manageable in a canoe locally, and goes on wilderness trips regularly in Killarney Park where nature, art and discovery meld. Mark has had a number of poems published in a variety of decent presses, as well as one poetry collection, TUG, published by Ars Omnia Press in 2016.

Greg Kennedy

*1. How would you describe your **relationship to the land**, and how long have you called a particular physical place 'home'?*

The Niagara escarpment was the first place where I truly felt a connection to the land. Growing up, I lived near Tew's Falls in Dundas, and walked along the Bruce Trail to school every day. Now, I live 60 km away from the Escarpment, at Ignatius Farm, but there is still a similar connection to the land for me here. The best word I can think of in terms of how I spend my time in the land is "contemplation." I spend time walking silently, taking everything in. Sitting, watching, being still, I can watch things happen, watch the stories of nature unfold. Animals, bugs, more distant stories of rock being formed by water: it all unfolds when approached with a spirit of contemplation. I find myself fascinated especially by the patience of water, the dance and intimacy of rock and water becoming, very slowly, something new.

*2. Is your relationship to the land affected by any particular **religious or spiritual grounding**, or does it come from a **specific worldview** of any kind?*

I once wanted to be a farmer, but found I wasn't called to it. Rather, I felt a religious curiosity, and as a result, arrived at Ignatius Farm. I see the Creator in all the nature around me—the fingerprints of God are all over the place in everything I see here. The spiritual connection to the land comes, in a sense, from a practical sensibility. I love this land in part for what it gives me—food, a place of light and repose, and a place that allows my imagination to amble around. I think about it this way: every person is lovable, but why do you fall in love with a certain person? And similarly with every piece of land: every ecosystem is lovable, so why do you fall in love with a certain one? I don't think that the land here has anything special except that there are many people who love it. Certainly it's pretty, but I think our individual interactions with the land are what make it so special. Every place is special if you allow it to be.

3. What is your ***motivation and hope in writing poetry*** *related to the environment? What kind of a role do you see poetry as fulfilling?*

For me, the hope of my poetry lies in the notion of ecological conversion. Conversion, to me, implies a wholesale change in one's being. Until we actually begin to have affection and see the land as part of our faith, part of our very selves, we aren't going to take care of it. It will become a concern of either economics or survival; it won't be a very deep or spiritual concern. If a change is made just out of fear or even aesthetics, it will be only temporary, it won't completely change a person. To write poetry is hoping to help in this conversion. And part of writing is my own conversion. You have to stop and look to write good poetry, otherwise you aren't really addressing what's there.

If I had to define God, I think I would define God as creativity. When I'm artistically creative, I feel that I'm participating in God somehow. Looking out of my window at a meadow, what's amazing about the creation of this place is that it doesn't create itself, it participates. It's the same with poetry. I try to slow down and open up, and something happens. I hope, through poetry, to get others to slow down and see things differently as well. There can be an edge to my poetry—not an aggression, I hope, but maybe a frustration, a prophetic frustration. I am hoping people will begin to notice the world all around us. I hope, through poetry, that I can be a part of some ecological conversion.

Greg Kennedy is the Executive Director of the Ignatius Jesuit Centre, just beyond the northern border of the city of Guelph. There he lives and works also as a spiritual director, which means he practices a good deal of intent listening. This, in fact, is how he approaches poetry—as an act of attuned listening.

He has published two academic books: *The Ontology of Trash: the disposable and its problematic nature* (2007) and *La cuidad penitente /The Penitent City* (2018), written in Spanish. Since then, *Amazing Friendships between Animals and Saints* and three volumes of *Reupholstered Psalms* have appeared. Central to his vocation are poetry and the Earth. He has lived and worked in Toronto, Ottawa, and Dundas, Ontario; Truro, Nova Scotia; St. Paul, Minnesota; Kingston, Jamaica; Vancouver, Edmonton; and Bogota and Pasto, Colombia.

Paula Kienapple-Summers

*1. How would you describe your **relationship to the land**, and how long have you called a particular physical place 'home'?*

I was born in Kitchener and have lived here all my life. My heritage is German: my Kienapple great-great grandparents settled in this area to farm. As a child, the area further outside my immediate neighbourhood was countryside or farms and we would bike out to explore and enjoy more open spaces. My current home is relatively close to the Grand River, which I've been familiar with my whole life. We have the Grand River Trail here in Kitchener/Waterloo which I hike on a regular basis. It's wonderful to see moving water within the city. There are different access points and the woodland trails are beautiful, easily accessible to the community, well maintained, and used by people of all different ages. When I was young, I didn't know that the land on each side of the Grand River (known as the Haldimand Tract) was negotiated in early treaties to be reserved for the Indigenous peoples. It's important to me to understand and acknowledge that where I live is their historic territory.

*2. Is your relationship to the land affected by any particular **religious or spiritual grounding**, or does it come from a **specific worldview** of any kind?*

For me, it's spiritually grounding to be out in nature, to be invited to walk along the river. When I see moving water, my problems seem to move away and be soothed. I feel a sense of peace there, being connected to something bigger than myself, a larger universe that is beautiful and wonderful and inexplicable and powerful—patient, ever-changing yet ever the same. As the seasons change and I change, the river is always flowing. Though I did have a traditional Christian upbringing, my spiritual connection with nature and that sense of wonder and awe is very strong within me.

3. What is your ***motivation and hope in writing poetry*** *related to the environment? What kind of a role do you see poetry as fulfilling?*

Poetry helps people connect, to get to the heart of emotions in very few words. In writing about the environment, my motivation is not only to be bring awareness of the physical environment but look at how it connects with us. In "Sunrise Over the Grand River," I was writing about how our city is interconnected to a beautiful landscape but also how we can forget that other creatures are living right here where our cars rumble over the river bridge day after day. I wanted to show how we can notice and appreciate nature every day on a commute, but also pose the difficult question: what happens when we encroach on nature? How can we live together with the ecosystems that the Grand River supports?

Paula Kienapple-Summers is a writer from Kitchener, Ontario. Her poems have appeared in literary journals including *Existere, The Nashwaak Review, Tower Poetry*, and *Spadina Literary Review*, as well as anthologies including *Voicing Suicide* (Ekstasis Press: 2020) and *Another Dysfunctional Cancer Poetry Anthology* (Mansfield Press: 2018). Email: tessera@golden.net

Gimaa (Chief) Stacey Laforme

*1. How would you describe your **relationship to the land**, and how long have you called a particular physical place 'home'?*

Well, my knowledge of [Mississauga] culture and history and the language was all but eroded because of where we lived and how close we are to Canadian society: at a point in our history we may have had one fluent speaker left, or maybe none that was fluent, and our culture was not practised anywhere. But I've always lived my life by certain beliefs and patterns, and I taught my children the same, and then when I was 50 years old I heard the [Anishinaabe] creation story being told, and I recognized that everything in my life and what I believed in was part of that creation story, so I recognized "that's where I come from, that's why I am who I am." Even though I never had anybody teach me any of the culture or the language or values and the way we lived, the connection I have with Mother Earth always existed inside me. And quite frankly when I write any poem I become the character in the poem: whether it's a tree, Mother Earth, or whoever it is, I become that character. That's how I write and how I express myself, so I live through every word I put on paper. It's not always easy for me, because some of the things I write about are very harsh and traumatic.

*2. Is your relationship to the land affected by any particular **religious or spiritual grounding**, or does it come from a **specific worldview** of any kind?*

It's hard to answer that specifically because I don't have any particular religious bent. I appreciate the value in the concept of religion trying to bring people together with love and hope—I respect that, and see it as an ally on some levels. But for myself, I guess I see it like this: people think that the world is so big, but it's not, it's tiny, it's a small little place compared to the universe—it's so small and the resources are limited, and nobody seems to understand that. It's not like people across the ocean are so far away—those are our neighbours! Those should be seen as our family and friends, or at least as our neighbours. When I talk about raising consciousness and awareness of the connection we all have to the planet, the universe, and everything else, that is a part of my belief system, and that affects how we relate to one another and to the world.

3. What is your ***motivation and hope in writing poetry*** *related to the environment? What kind of a role do you see poetry as fulfilling?*

When you say "poetry related to the environment," I don't view things that way—I understand loving Mother Earth and that we need to heal and respect her, but we're also talking about the waters, the plants, the birds, the animals, ourselves: it's all interconnected. So when I talk about the environment in my writing, I always talk about it in the context of the people, and how we relate not only to the planet but to each other: that's fundamental.

Art is such a bridge between worlds and understanding. It doesn't have to be poetry—it can be song, music, dance: whatever it is, it connects people on a much deeper level than just facts and figures do. And that is so important when you're trying to make a difference. I think artists have an obligation to try and make the world a little better, and through their art they can do that— raising consciousness, making people more aware. I once said at an event that it won't be the politicians and warriors who decide the future of this world, it will be the singers, the dancers, the drummers, the poets, the storytellers—it will be artists who determine where we go in this world, and where our future lies.

What we really need is a fundamental shift in the way we view the world around us, our place within it, and each other—that's what's got to be the next evolutionary step. I wrote one poem, "Climate Change?", just so I could say the lines "Instead of thinking that climate change / is a problem to be solved, / Think instead of Mother Earth / as a soul to be saved." The hope I have for the future is, if we can do that, we can do anything. You can't make that little shift without it affecting your life personally, how you interact with family and friends, because it's all connected. If we just have that shift in understanding, that's how we save the world. Many people will tell you the next great invention or the next great AI system is what can help you, but the only way to really help us is for humanity to change the way we view things.

Gimaa (Chief) R. Stacey Laforme was elected Chief of the Mississaugas of the Credit First Nation in 2015, and served in that position until 2023. His love for the Mississaugas' treaty lands, and all the people living in those lands, is widely recognized. In 2017, he became only the third Honorary Senior Fellow of Massey College, Toronto, alongside the Duke of Edinburgh and the Chancellor of Oxford University. He recently led a delegation to the U.K., and became the first Chief to meet with the British monarch in over 160 years. He has published two volumes of poetry with UpRoute/Durvile Publications, *Living in the Tall Grass: Poems of Reconciliation* (2017) and *Love Life Loss and a little bit of hope: Poems from the Soul* (2024).

Janice Jo Lee

1. How would you describe your ***relationship to the land****, and how long have you called a particular physical place 'home'?*

I wish I was closer to the land. I was born in downtown Toronto, and when there's concrete I feel like the land is covered; there's a barrier between me and the land. The manicured trees on sidewalks are built around like they're inconveniences—rather than the buildings being inconveniences placed on top of the land. That grieves me.

I identify Kitchener-Waterloo as my home because I lived there through my formative years as a youth, in becoming an artist, and in really exploring community in relation to the land. Having picnics in Waterloo Park, for example, or biking to Victoria Park and having formative memories under specific trees. Or at Silver Lake in Waterloo Park, memories with my friends on that dock, singing with guitars with the water right in front of us, and the geese, and the goose poo—everything that comes with it. I have stories, songs, poems, and specific memories tied to these geographical features of KW—on bike rides to Elora Gorge, bike rides down to the Grand River. I have been a part of helping land defenders protesting Line 9, and community formed around that.

I moved from KW to my dream area of Toronto, right beside High Park, with my dog. I spent the first four months just walking in High Park on the west side, in the forest trails by Grenadier pond, and that was real medicine. The land loves you back, right? Watching the flowers come up, the trees become green, and coming back to a sense of wonder—a capacity for gratitude.

2. Is your relationship to the land affected by any particular ***religious or spiritual grounding****, or does it come from a* ***specific worldview*** *of any kind?*

Well, I grew up Catholic and went to mass every Sunday till the end of grade twelve. A teaching I remember learning in high school, from my religion teacher, was our responsibility to be stewards of the land. There are specific ideas I keep although I don't identify as a Catholic anymore, ones that were foundational in forming my values and worldview. I've been more in touch with Indigenous teachings in recent years. I've been doing arts education with Indigenous organizations. It really works for me, the storytelling ways of some of the wampum belts like One Dish One Spoon. If the land is a dish, and there's only one spoon, we all have to share it; we all have to take turns using the spoon. Metaphor, for me as a poet, makes it so much easier to understand. All my latest writing, in the last five years, deeply uses nature metaphor and imagery.

3. What is your ***motivation and hope in writing poetry*** *related to the environment? What kind of a role do you see poetry as fulfilling?*

I identify as a folk artist, and I think a good folk artist can write pieces that are timeless: true now, true a hundred years ago, true in a hundred years. I always say that the best way to do that is to use nature metaphors. Because hopefully there will still be trees in a hundred years! In general, the human experience around the world understands what water is, what the sky is, and the birds—nature imagery helps make ideas universally comprehensible.

I'm interested in poetry that stops us. Poetry as resistance to the capitalism which propels us to be "productive," and "grow the economy," as opposed to what I think poetry can do in its best form, which is to practice gratitude, wonder, and perspective. There's also, of course, the pain-aspect of what poetry can capture. It's not meant to deny life, but to affirm it. I don't necessarily like the word *capture*; poetry doesn't capture—poetry conveys, poetry illuminates.

Janice Jo Lee (she/they) 이승혜 is an award-winning queer multidisciplinary artist based in Tkaronto, Ontario. She is a second-generation Canadian settler and twenty-seventh generation Korean. She is a contemporary folk singer, songwriter, composer, sound designer, spoken word poet, actor, clown, satirist, and educator, as well as a nationally-touring independent musician and bandleader. Her latest album *Ancestor Song* is a testament to healing and remembering your roots. janicejolee.ca

John B. Lee

*1. How would you describe your **relationship to the land**, and how long have you called a particular physical place 'home'?*

The first seventeen years of my life were spent being raised on a fifth-generation farm in southwestern Ontario, in Kent County, near the end of the Underground Railway. My original relationship with the land was as a farm boy, brought up with the family farm tradition, living in harmony with the land and leaving it better than you found it. I went to London for university; after that I moved with my wife to Brantford for twenty years, and from there to the vibrant commercial fishing town of Port Dover, where I am now living in a lake house overlooking Long Point Bay on the south coast of Lake Erie.

But I would call "home" where the heart is. I have many homes—some of them are in recollection. You can be at home if you're centred, wherever you are. As long as some part of you touches the ground, you can be at home, you can build a connection—that feeling of being awake and alive where you are. You can also leave a place without leaving it—you carry with you the places that you love.

*2. Is your relationship to the land affected by any particular **religious or spiritual grounding**, or does it come from a **specific worldview** of any kind?*

My religious background was in an Anglican village church; at one point I was so serious about it that I thought maybe someday I would be a minister, but when I became a server I realized that I was too in love with the trappings, and that meant I was thinking of the wrong vocation. I have a deep connection to what I learned through Christian teachings, but a

2,000-year-old tradition seems very new, when you think about the much longer time that humans had been around before that, apparently without a messiah.

The idea of spirit, having a spiritual connection between yourself and the universe, yourself and the ground, comes from a feeling of not being alienated, not having a sense of otherness between yourself and the external world. I edited an anthology* with Brother Paul Quenon, a Trappist monk, in which I wanted to try to build a community where a spiritual atheist and a true believer could find common ground. I want every poem to have the head, the heart, the body, the soul, and the Spirit: the rational, the emotional that's interconnected with all life, the physical with its joys and sorrows, and some kind of deep sense that you were always here—something that is connected to the Spirit that is outside of you. Everything begins on the earth; gravity holds you here, to this earth and all of its wonders. To feel that connection harmoniously between all five elements is my worldview. And the idea of agreeing to try to understand the other point of view seems key to me. Our culture tends to emphasize alienation and otherness, but I'm drawn to the idea of a harmonious union of two diversities, not even requiring complete unity. What do you lose and what do you gain, when one culture comes into contact with another culture? I have a natural predisposition toward harmony, perhaps because my paternal family was materialistic and intellectual, but my maternal family was about love of family: those two very different perspectives enabled me to have profound affection for the idea that you're here for other people, for difference.

3. What is your ***motivation and hope in writing poetry*** *related to the environment? What kind of a role do you see poetry as fulfilling?*

The wonderful thing about surrendering to the muse is getting rid of the ego. I write poetry in order to get out of the way; I didn't know I knew some of the things that the poem teaches me. I write poetry because I know the feeling of when it's done well, of vanishing into the work and drawing from the deep inner wells of the self, where the water is clear. In

---

* *Smaller Than God* (Black Moss Press, 2002)

our culture there's a certain kind of ugly energy in chaos and negativity, and we're drawn to it like moths to a flame—but *thanatos* and *eros* are complementary. I want the reader to experience a celebration of life and the life-force, of love and positivity—of Mother Earth.

I've been struck by how many poets have written about the post-glacial landscape of this area, the strata and substrata. I love the words about this landscape: esker, moraine, drumlin, glacial teardrop—wonderful words! And a single word can be the source of a thousand thoughts: it can unlock a whole universe, a whole history of communities over time.

John B. Lee was appointed Poet Laureate of the city of Brantford in perpetuity in 2004 and Poet Laureate of Norfolk County for life in 2015. He is also Poet Laureate of the Canada Cuba Literary Alliance (2020-2022). With seventy-five books in print, his work has appeared internationally in over five hundred publications, and he is the recipient of over one hundred writing awards, including the 2021 Arthur Lefebvre Award for Excellence in Career Achievement by a Brantford Writer (Brantford Writers' Circle). He lives in a lake house overlooking Long Point Bay on the south coast of Lake Erie in the town of Port Dover, where he works as a full-time author.

Sheryl Loeffler (1949-2024)

1. How would you describe your **relationship to the land***, and how long have you called a particular physical place 'home'?*

In an old *Jack Benny Program* rerun, Jack Benny describes himself as a "cliff dweller" because he lives in a high-rise. So do I. I've lived on the top floor of a condo at the top of a hill in Waterloo for the last 30 years. My apartment has two enclosed balconies. I see sunrises every morning from the living room balcony and sunsets every evening from the bedroom balcony. I know the sky. I watch storms rolling in. I watch birds—crows, doves, geese, seagulls, turkey vultures, among the larger birds. Sometimes migrating geese fly so close I feel as if I could touch them. I know the land through windows, too. Because I'm on the eleventh floor, I get extraordinary views across Waterloo Region. It's amazing how forested it is. It's absolutely lovely watching the seasons change. I've taken many, many photographs from my balconies.

And though I don't feel an intimate connection to the land here, there are places in the world where I've taken the land into my heart: the Appalachian foothills of my mother's hometown on the Ohio River, where Ohio meets Kentucky and West Virginia; Italy, my husband's and my travel destination for ten years, where we rented farmhouses looking out over fields of sunflowers and vineyards of grapes; Arkansas—to my surprise—where I lived at a writers' colony in the wooded Ozarks for two months in 2017; and the little island archipelago of Malta, at the heart of the Mediterranean Sea, where the weather patterns are more African than European, with its dusty brown garigue punctuated by neon bougainvillea, yellow- and pink-flowering cactus, carob and broad-leafed fig trees, orange hibiscuses, deep pink

Judas trees, purple jacarandas, and white, pink, and red oleander. My husband and I lived there for a year and returned once or twice a year for the next 12 years.

2. Is your relationship to the land affected by any particular ***religious or spiritual grounding****, or does it come from a* ***specific worldview*** *of any kind?*

The short answers to the two parts of the question are No and No. However, when I walk Waterloo's beautiful wooded trails, I feel decompression, calming, healing.

I had an almost religious experience at one of Malta's unroofed Neolithic temples. Ġgantija (built between 3600 and 3200 BCE) was carpeted in rainy winter green, dotted with yellow cape sorrel. When I walked in, I felt as if I had entered sacred space.

3. What is your ***motivation and hope in writing poetry*** *related to the environment? What kind of a role do you see poetry as fulfilling?*

The poems I submitted are part of a nine-poem series I called *Roadsides, Woods, and Waste Places*, which is where wildflowers grow. My motivation in writing them was to explore my admittedly limited relationship with nature. I wrote about wildflowers that evoked memories or associations in me.

I don't believe, with Shelley, that poets are "the unacknowledged legislators of the world." I don't believe that poets can establish legal (or moral) norms in civil society. But they can articulate them. In that sense, imaginative practice and political activism can wed. I must say, however—I dislike political rants.

For me, writing poetry is knocking the heads of disparate ideas together, playing with words. I don't think of poetry as "having a role"; I think of it, rather, as being an experience. Stephen Spender defined poetry as "a use of language which reveals external actuality as symbolic inner consciousness," bringing the inside out and the outside in. I'd like my poems to be places of congruity between my readers and me, where my memories of or associations with, in this case, wildflowers (or other poetic subjects) can be understood and shared.

It is with great sadness that we report that Sheryl Loeffler died suddenly on January 12, 2024, just as our collection was on the final stretch towards getting published. We have left her interview and biographical note as she wrote them. May her poems indeed be places of congruity between her readers and her.

Sheryl Loeffler usually describes herself as a musician and writer. She had a 45-year career as a church musician in five local congregations, and has held writing jobs at Wilfrid Laurier University and YW Kitchener-Waterloo. Her poetry, prose poetry, and creative non-fiction have been published in Canada, the USA, the UK, Austria, and Japan. In 2014, her book *A Land in the Storytelling Sea*, born in and about Malta, was published by FARAXA Publishing, Rabat, Malta. In 2015, she was elected to membership in the League of Canadian Poets. In 2017, she was resident at The Writers' Colony at Dairy Hollow, Eureka Springs, Arkansas, USA. In 2019, she was nominated for a Pushcart Prize.

Tanis MacDonald

1. How would you describe your ***relationship to the land****, and how long have you called a particular physical place 'home'?*

I've lived in Southern Ontario since 2006, and before that, I lived all over Canada. Because Ontario isn't the place I would define first and foremost as my home place, I would say that I'm still negotiating what it means to be here. My family in Manitoba were working-class farmers, and I was the first person in my family to get a graduate degree. For a long time, I eschewed having a relationship with the land—I was far too intellectual for that! The older I got, however, the more I understood that this was not a matter of class, nor of proving myself as an intellectual, but more like a vital way to be in the world. Modernity puts a lot of effort into convincing us that place doesn't matter: that one place is very much like any other. It's a huge concern of globalism and the global economy to wipe away the specificities of place. I think, though, that it's really necessary to people's well-being to connect with nature and to have a sense of place.

2. Is your relationship to the land affected by any particular ***religious or spiritual grounding****, or does it come from a* ***specific worldview*** *of any kind?*

When you grow up in Southern Manitoba, not everybody farms, but everybody has a relationship with farmers; it's a very agriculturally centered place. My parents both grew up in very small towns just north of the North Dakota border, a place with lots of Indigenous people, lots of Mennonite people, lots of Ukrainian people, and lots of Scottish/Irish/English people like my parents. I'd call this a cultural-spiritual grounding because my grandparents, with spectacular bad timing, immigrated to Canada just in time for the Depression, with the promise of land that they couldn't get in the U.K. Then suddenly, the land wasn't feeding anybody, and their relationship with the land became a kind of bartered one. I inherited this idea that the land is what feeds us—food doesn't come from nowhere, it comes from the ground. It's something I absorbed despite the fact that I, too, grew up in modernity. It's not like I dodged the influence of the modern era—I spent an adolescence trying to get away from those ideas, and put myself in the world of books. But looking back on cultural traditions that tell us the practical ways to be in the world, and noting what is around us and our dependence on the land, is important. For me, this cultural background has become a kind of spiritual understanding.

*3. What is your **motivation and hope in writing poetry** related to the environment? What kind of a role do you see poetry as fulfilling?*

I write in order to figure things out. In making my writing public, I'm not only saying "Here's me trying to figure out a difficult idea" but I'm also saying "Am I crazy? Does anyone else notice this?" I hope to bring together natural language and language that is not very natural at all, and I think those are two ways out of hundreds of seeing, not easily split between an urban and a natural way. We shouldn't pretend we don't see the natural and the urban blending, because we see them together all the time. We have parks in cities, and provincial parks with buildings in them, and everything in between. I'm interested in that meeting of elements, and in having people encounter the land around them.

Tanis MacDonald (she/they) is the author of *Straggle: Adventures in Walking While Female, Mobile: poems, The Daughter's Way,* and four other books. With Ariel Gordon, Tanis co-edited the special "Moving on Land" issue of *The Goose* (2023). Tanis serves as the General Editor of the Laurier Poetry Series and hosts the podcast *Watershed Writers*. She has twice been longlisted for the CBC Poetry Prize. Tanis is a Professor in the Department of English and Film Studies at Wilfrid Laurier University, situated on traditional Haudenosaunee territory in the Grand River watershed.

Daniel MacIsaac

1. How would you describe your ***relationship to the land****, and how long have you called a particular physical place 'home'?*

For me a relationship with the land is reciprocal—we belong to the land and the land belongs to us. I was born in Nanaimo, have spent a lot of my life there, and have always felt very attached to the west coast. My kids spent much time outdoors in nature, so they increased my attachment to the lands and seas and lakes around us here on Vancouver Island. Over about ten years, my wife and I also lived off and on in Toronto, including in an apartment on College Drive while our kids attended Canada's National Ballet School, and we explored Halton. We have relatives with a cottage just outside Toronto so we spent a lot of time there, going on canoeing trips and exploring the ecosystems around the Golden Horseshoe, and whenever things got too much we got out to the Toronto islands. Toronto is a kind of second home.

2. Is your relationship to the land affected by any particular ***religious or spiritual grounding****, or does it come from a* ***specific worldview*** *of any kind?*

I was raised in a time when everyone went to church, and our family was a "small" Catholic family (there were only 7 children, barely enough to fill one pew!). What I have an affinity for after all this time is Celtic Christianity, with its reverence for the spiritual found in natural elements. My ancestors were Gaelic speakers who were cleared in 1792 from South Uist in the Hebrides, so I feel a real affinity with South Uist and Iona. I've also done some reading of the *Carmina Gadelica* with its hymns and prayers translated and collected by Alexander Carmichael. Mary Oliver has an essay called

"Winter Hours" that says what is important in life and for your attention is finding the spiritual in the physical, and she says elsewhere that we all have a third self that has a hunger for eternity. What amazes me about Mary Oliver is that it seems from reading her poetry that she walked out every morning and experienced eternity, and I think, "I would like to achieve that more than once a decade," that deep connection and immersion. That's what my hunger is which hasn't been satisfied. But I certainly aspire to experience the infinite more often, more intensely.

3. What is your ***motivation and hope in writing poetry*** *related to the environment? What kind of a role do you see poetry as fulfilling?*

Poetry is of course very personal, yet poets are always looking for an audience. And whenever there is a transformative event happening, it seems that poetry is part of it. I can give an example here on the west coast: when the Clayoquot protests and blockades occurred in the early '90s to preserve old growth, poetry and lyrical music had a big role in galvanizing people and helping them coalesce as a group. Now we have the Fairy Creek protests carrying on, and there's been poetry and song, drumming, and gathering outside the legislature by Indigenous and non-Indigenous people. So I think poetry has a significant galvanizing role to play in transforming society and preserving the environment.

For ten years, **Dan MacIsaac** served as a director on UVIC's Environmental Law Centre board. He has travelled in the wild places of southern Ontario. Brick Books published his collection of poetry, *Cries from the Ark*. His poetry has received awards, including, for "Paul on the Adriatic," the 2014 Foley Prize from *America Magazine*. In 2022, Alfred Gustav published his chapbook, *Jazz Sessions*. His work has been short-listed for the Walrus Poetry Prize, The Nick Blatchford Occasional Verse Contest, and the CBC Short Story Prize.

Chandra F. Maracle

*1. How would you describe your **relationship to the land**, and how long have you called a particular physical place 'home'?*

I grew up on the West Side of Buffalo, New York, so that will always be home for me. We also had a home in Fort Erie where I spent a lot of time growing up, so that also feels like home. If I am asked where I'm from, I can answer in many ways. If you're asking where I was born and raised, I would say Buffalo. If a Haudenosaunee person is asking, meaning what homeland territory, I would say Kenhte:ke or Tyendinaga. I've also been living at Six Nations of the Grand River for eighteen years. To come from, or be from, a place can be a complicated matter.

Then there's the idea of relating to the land itself. I can walk down a city street and feel as connected to it as when I'm outside our home at Six Nations, where there's nothing but trees for acres. It's fascinating to me that I can find the same medicine that grows in my yard, also growing through the cracks of the sidewalk in Buffalo. We have this mistaken idea that people who live in the country are automatically more connected to the land, but if you look at the Haudenosaunee Thanksgiving address, and all the things that are acknowledged in that worldview, you can see that everyone is dependent on the earth. Even if you just focus on the sky, you'll find out that we're all connected to it, no matter where you're from.

*2. Is your relationship to the land affected by any particular **religious or spiritual grounding**, or does it come from a **specific worldview** of any kind?*

Most of the people I know who are around my age did not grow up in a traditional Haudenosaunee environment. I was a kid who always had a spiritual sense, but I didn't really learn about the spiritual and then ceremonial context of things until I was in my late teens, and at around 23 that fell into place. I always knew there was something more to life, and Longhouse ceremonies just put that into practice for me. It's hard for me to talk about things without my spirituality coming through, because I have been marinating in it for the past thirty years.

One of the biggest ways in which my spiritual grounding affects my relationship to the earth is in the idea that everything is connected to everything else. My spirituality is not separate from my ideas about food or my relationship to the land, but intertwined with it. In Haudenosaunee cosmology, it's nearly impossible to talk about the Earth without referring to her as our Mother, and that makes a difference in how we see and, hopefully, treat her. The cosmos takes on a deeper meaning as you look at Haudenosaunee cosmology, because we see that we're related to the things we can see in the sky and those we can't see on the other side of the sky. The Creation story tells us that when we die, our souls become stars. We can look up there and find comfort in knowing that's where our family relations are.

3. What is your ***motivation and hope in writing poetry*** *related to the environment? What kind of a role do you see poetry as fulfilling?*

I think we should all read more poetry. I think we should all write more poetry. Language is so powerful. In a Haudenosaunee context, we most often begin our gatherings with some words that acknowledge our collective humanity. As part of my PhD work, I was writing about Haudenosaunee food history and how it can transform our relationship with food. I am a holistic thinker by nature, probably because of my arts-based education, and I know that everything is related to everything else. Seeing the world through the eyes of an artist for me means that I see the artistic and creative and spiritual in it all. I was looking at food, yet I kept coming back to the opening words of Haudenosaunee gatherings. I was reminded of the power of words and being a good speaker, and that is an old Haudenosaunee value. Thinking through these ideas, I decided that I should open my paper with some of my own words as a recognition of the eater in all of us. That poem ended up being part of the introduction to my paper, because of the way it highlights the collective, worldwide grief we experience surrounding food and our disconnection from its source. I would like people who read my poem to see that they have a relationship to food that is spiritual by nature, and that this is nothing to be afraid of. I want people to remember that life can be delicious whether you're eating it or reading it.

Chandra Maracle is Kanyen'keha:ka/Mohawk Nation and she lives at Six Nations of the Grand River Territory. She has four daughters and wears many hats. She is currently a PhD student in the Faculty of Environmental Studies at York University. She is researching Haudenosaunee (Six Nations) food history, eating psychology and postpartum food and care practices. Email: cfmaracle2@aol.com

Kate Marshall Flaherty

1. How would you describe your ***relationship to the land****, and how long have you called a particular physical place 'home'?*

My relationship to the land is deep, and in every fiber of my being. I need to walk in nature every day, like a dog! The rhythm of my body, the movement of the seasons, the birds, and everything—are integral to my daily practice, health, and wellbeing.

There are three places that are dear to me on this planet. The first is the Georgian Bay area where my parents have a farm, and where I worked at Killbear Provincial Park. We would whack the dirt off carrots for dinner and go get an egg warm from under "the ladies" in the barn. Then as a young adult, I left my father's house and had my right of passage in the Rockies. I was also blessed as a writer and yogi to travel, for the last several years, with [the writing organization] Inkslingers. I would teach yoga and guide writing workshops in Ireland, the place of my ancestors and my history.

2. Is your relationship to the land affected by any particular ***religious or spiritual grounding****, or does it come from a* ***specific worldview*** *of any kind?*

I was raised in the Catholic Christian tradition as a child, loving particularly Saint Francis, Saint Clare, Mary Oliver, John O'Donohue, and creation stories and myths. Things like "consider the lilies" resonated with me. Many yoga poses, too, are connected to animals and our place in nature. To me, creation is the holy book; it teaches us. I taught world religions in high schools for twelve years, and in every spiritual tradition there are "green rules," if you will. Codes of ethics, reciprocity with nature, healing properties of nature. We're most at ease and healed when we're connected to nature, and we get disconnected and broken when we wander from, abuse, or overtax nature. We're a part of the earth, and the earth is a part of us. My overarching belief is divine healing light in all things: in the earth, in all beings, in every river, rabbit, person—even a person with whom I don't agree!

3. What is your ***motivation and hope in writing poetry*** *related to the environment? What kind of a role do you see poetry as fulfilling?*

Poets are prophets, witnesses to beauty and truth, and advocates giving voice to the voiceless. The trees can't speak, water can't speak, fish can't speak … Our role is to celebrate and to advocate. Sometimes it's as simple as holding a mirror to the beauty of nature to help people stop and notice, and sometimes it's to talk about our detrimental effect on our planet, our home, and what we can do to change it. My poetry has become more urgent, possibly more challenging, and certainly more political because of climate change.

As poets we look to our place in the cosmos. In one way, it's a pinprick in this huge, interconnected web, but in another way, the only lens I know is through my poet-vision. My favourite quote from Mary Oliver says, "It's not what the words say, it's how they make you feel." If it's an Athabasca poem and you feel the glacial ice, the steam, and are aware that it has receded more in the last thirty years than it did in thirty centuries—that's what we want to feel. We want the reader to reach these conclusions by what they feel, rather than by being told.

Kate Marshall Flaherty most recently published *Titch* (Piquant Press, 2023) and *Digging* (Aeolus House, 2022). She was shortlisted for *Tifferet's* Spiritual Poetry Prize 2020, The Mitchell Poetry Prize 2021, *Arc's* Poem of the Year 2019, and the Gwendolyn MacEwen Poetry Prize 2018. All her poems explore our interconnectedness—with the earth, each other, and the creator of all. See her performance poetry at https://katemarshallflaherty.ca.

Geoff Martin

*1. How would you describe your **relationship to the land**, and how long have you called a particular physical place 'home'?*

After twenty years living elsewhere in Ontario (London, Hamilton) or in Costa Rica, South Korea, and in various places throughout the United States, I returned a few years ago to live in the Grand River watershed, within the Haldimand Tract, where I grew up. I'll likely now call Waterloo Region home for the rest of my life.

Despite all that itinerant movement—or maybe because of it—my writing has often grappled with ideas of home and belonging and with the complicated land histories and settlement stories that have structured my relations to this place since childhood. And it's through writing and reading, listening and walking, that I am seeking to simultaneously learn and unlearn my various gendered, ethnic, religious, racial, geographic, ecological and embodied relationships to the land. It's a lifelong project, obviously.

It's also worth noting that places are never static and that no two places are exactly alike either. I might have returned to this watershed, but it's true that you can't go home again, not really. More to the point, I live now in the city of Kitchener, which is a different sort of place from my hometown of Elmira. As a result, I feel quite new here, and I'm still actively feeling my way around this place, seeking to learn it anew.

*2. Is your relationship to the land affected by any particular **religious or spiritual grounding**, or does it come from a **specific worldview** of any kind?*

I am increasingly attuned to the ways in which the land is foundational and teeming with life. The land, along with the air and the water, are the essential matter—the literal ground—in which I "live and move and have my being."

That phrasing, borrowed over from the Acts of the Apostles, also names a tradition. My relationship to land has been profoundly shaped by various Christian religious ideas about the Earth as both a gift from God and as "ours" to subdue and dominate. I am Mennonite by ancestry and by present religious affiliation, which connects me to a long theological and social tradition that seeks to live humbly or "quiet in the land." It's also a tradition that, contradictorily, boasts (and bemoans) largescale agrarian land transformations all over the world. Whether along the Upper Grand of Ontario, or across the Midwestern prairies of Canada and the United States, or in the Ukrainian Steppe, the Paraguayan Chaco, the valleys of Northern Mexico etc. etc., Mennonite communal settlement has often served as the vanguard for colonization and resource extraction following the dispossession of Indigenous people from their lands. Farming, in other words, in secondary service to empire.

It's a complicated legacy to carry. If I was any good at selling tractors, I'd likely be a fourth-generation farm machinery dealer. Instead, I'm writing about these affiliations and traditions, trying to understand myself in place and time, and trying to live into my responsibilities to the damaged land I call home.

3. What is your ***motivation and hope in writing poetry*** *related to the environment? What kind of a role do you see poetry as fulfilling?*

My motivation to write poetry and lyric essays in response to "nature" as well as to the social and environmental histories of a given place is informed significantly by the process and posture the work requires. The daily tasks of journaling, drafting, and revising serve to slow me down. They make me pay closer attention than I might otherwise offer the world around me. It's this attention that matters, more than the words.

I often think about Simone Weil's line that "absolutely unmixed attention is prayer." It names a kind of prayer that neither asks nor demands but listens. Wonder and horror are both intrinsic to this orientation. To write with and about land and air and water during the Anthropocene is to bear witness to both the burning world and to forms of life that are still, somehow, persisting and adapting. I want to participate in that work of attending to a very small but meaningful fraction of the Earth's ten trillion particularities.

Geoff Martin's place-based and environmental essays have been nominated twice for the Pushcart Prize and have appeared in *The New Quarterly, Creative Nonfiction, Literary Review of Canada, Boulevard*, and *The Common*, among others. He holds an M.A. from McMaster University and is currently completing an essay collection—called *Homeground*—with funding support from the Canada Council for the Arts, the Ontario Arts Council, and the Region of Waterloo Arts Fund.

Elizabeth McCallister

1. How would you describe your ***relationship to the land****, and how long have you called a particular physical place 'home'?*

I'm a typical old-fashioned Canadian settler. On my mother's side I'm French-Canadian—we go back to one of the first boats that arrived in Canada; on my dad's side—he's a first-generation Canadian from Ireland. I grew up in Scarborough; I went to high-school in the Beaches, and used to hang out down in the ravine there. Then when my husband was doing his doctorate, we spent seven years in Saskatoon, a very different kind of environment—it looked pretty empty! Much darker in the winter, much longer days in the summer, gophers, shorter trees, and much flatter country of course. And then back to Kitchener for two or three years, and from there to Brantford, where we've lived now for 16 years. The river trails are a great way to get to calming pockets of nature, even in the city. I'm most connected to urban nature; for me, nature is always tied to humans, and how humans are interacting with the natural environment, or too often causing damage to it.

2. Is your relationship to the land affected by any particular ***religious or spiritual grounding****, or does it come from a* ***specific worldview*** *of any kind?*

I don't have a romantic view of the natural world: the cheetah is always going to catch the baby gazelle. But my spontaneous response to nature is just to enjoy it, to respond with the senses, to have meditative moments. In a wider worldview, I do believe in God, and that we've been handed the earth as a gift to keep in good order for future generations. I feel badly that we've abused it, and so many of its people, so badly: I think that makes for a very dire spiritual emergency that we do need to address.

3. What is your ***motivation and hope in writing poetry*** *related to the environment? What kind of a role do you see poetry as fulfilling?*

I've been called an urban poet. I don't see myself as just a nature poet, but I do see poetry as important in recording what we see now, what we know now, what we feel now. So looking at nature now, as degraded or preserved, is something people will want to know about in the future. In my poetry I imagine I'm talking to the future unknown—I'm always writing to the reader in the dark future. There's this longing to connect, trying to make us understand each other a bit better. I want people to notice and appreciate the specifics of what happens in the natural world, and perhaps to learn from it about self-giving.

Elizabeth McCallister grew up in Scarborough and attended a high school in the Beaches neighbourhood, where she learned to appreciate nature within an urban setting. She moved with her husband to Saskatoon to complete his PhD in history, and then back to Ontario, first to Kitchener and then to Brantford. She has been described as an "urban poet, which doesn't mean a lack of appreciation for nature or the environment which surrounds all of us. There are pockets all arounds us just waiting to be noticed—a well-landscaped front yard, a ravine below Kingston Road, or a grassy lot where gophers hang out." Her work has appeared in *Hearthbeat: Poems of Family and Hometown, The World Around Us* chapbook, *Tamaracks: Canadian poetry for the 21st century*, and *Voices Israel 2021 Poetry Anthology*, as well as in other anthologies. Email: elizabethmccallister@sympatico.ca

Daniel David Moses (1952-2020)

*1. How would you describe your **relationship to the land**, and how long have you called a particular physical place 'home'?*

If a sense of the environment is in my work, it's because of my background. I grew up on a dairy farm with plenty of woodlots adjoining our fields, so work or play, I lived with and in the natural world and got experience of how it functioned. On top of that, the farm was on the Six Nations Reserve, and the largely unarticulated traditional culture of the community probably also shaped my unconscious sensibility.

*2. Is your relationship to the land affected by any particular **religious or spiritual grounding**, or does it come from a **specific worldview** of any kind?*

I was raised Anglican, that imported set of traditions, so we didn't talk about "pagan" things [i.e. Six Nations traditional culture]. But I feel that I use my writing as a sort of spiritual practise, so it's not a way to contribute to thought in our materialistic culture. Maybe what I do is a sort of written refuge or sanctuary for the awe or at least wonder I've sussed out of the natural world? It's a weird comfort that we need the world but it doesn't really need us. Creation will go on without us—

*3. What is your **motivation and hope in writing poetry** related to the environment? What kind of a role do you see poetry as fulfilling?*

So few people read or can read poetry in this culture. It's taught as if it's an intellectual puzzle instead of a human expression of the complexity of life. "What's the poet really mean?" If there were a way to say it in other words, the poet would have used them. I always try to be very present when I'm doing readings. My aesthetic, such as it is, keeps spoken or performed language in mind. The human experience mixes emotional or social dimensions to articulate the spiritual or human meaning. Prose tries for some appearance of objectivity. If I wanted to focus on issues, I'd probably be writing non-fiction or at least some kind of prose. Poetry needs to be seen as a thing complete in itself and not simply agitprop. Agitprop is its own thing … I think poetry is about the complicated combination of emotion and thought in art that creates a morality, a moral vision of the world, and that it's really the deepest way you can think.

We acknowledge with deep sadness that ***Daniel David Moses*** *died during the early days of the compilation of this anthology, on July 13, 2020. This interview summary has been constructed largely from comments he made to the editors by email, August 30, 2017; the final sentence is a quote from a previous interview with him, published in Canadian Literature, Jan. 29, 2015.*

Daniel David Moses's obituary, published by RHB Anderson Funeral Homes, July 2020, pointed out that "Daniel acknowledged his Delaware Nation paternal lineage while also embracing his maternal lineage in the Tuscarora Nation, Bear Clan." Moses was a playwright and poet who grew up on a farm on the Six Nations lands on the Grand River near Brantford. He published five volumes of poetry and six plays, for which he won numerous awards, including the 2001 Harbourfront Festival Prize and a 2003 Chalmers Arts Fellowship. One of his most recent poems in this anthology, "Some Grand River Blues," comes from *River Range: Poems*, a 2012 CD with original music by David DeLeary. Until his retirement in 2019, Moses had for twenty-five years taught drama at Queen's University in Kingston, ON.

Honey Novick

1. How would you describe your ***relationship to the land****, and how long have you called a particular physical place 'home'?*

I've been speaking for the environment for decades, because I'm a steward. I am equally respectful to the land of maple trees and snow as I am to the land of sand and palm-trees. I'm the daughter of immigrants from Palestine/Israel, but I was born and raised in Toronto; as an adult I spent many years going back and forth to California and to New York, but Toronto is my home. I love Hamilton too: Poets for Peace started there, an organization I wrote poems for, and I still make regular pilgrimages to the Royal Botanical Gardens. For years I've also been very involved in poetry and music in Guelph: I followed a fox who led me into the ruins in Erin Mills, and there I found a flyer which introduced me to the Guelph poetry and jazz festival! Later I created a poetry festival to happen on Canada Day at McCrae House in Guelph, so that poetry and McCrae would still be celebrated together.

2. Is your relationship to the land affected by any particular ***religious or spiritual grounding****, or does it come from a* ***specific worldview*** *of any kind?*

My appreciation for the natural world began for me as an only child: the flowers and animals and butterflies were my friends. As an adult I came to have a very strong awareness of both the physical and the invisible connections between one place and another. Wherever I am, it's the artists, the dreamers, who speak to the invisible powers at work in the trees and all living beings. Though my background is Jewish, I'm a practicing Nichiren Buddhist. I learned to chant "Nam Myoho Renge Kyo"[53] through some very difficult times in my life; through chanting I'm aware that I am not the centre of the universe, but I have a spiritual connection to everything else. I'm aware of the tides, of bird migration, of the sounds that animals make. It's the invisible energy that needs to be spoken about—it's alive but invisible.

3. What is your ***motivation and hope in writing poetry*** *related to the environment? What kind of a role do you see poetry as fulfilling?*

My training is as a vocalist at the Royal Conservatory; early on, I volunteered at the Mariposa Folk Festival, where I was assigned to what they called the "Native section," and I met First Nations musicians and Inuit throat-singers. We connected heart-to-heart. And afterwards I signed up to learn Ojibway! That introduced me to a whole culture that I feel needs to be more prevalent.

My songs and poems give me many things. They become like a friend, like a child, like a dream, like a call to arms. If I'm granted words that can express a feeling that has respect for everybody, then I want it to be clear. What I say has to be sincere, there has to be truth to it, an understanding that we live in a bigger world than just our little piece; there has to be reverence that accepts grace and beauty everywhere. Back in the '70s there was an activist movement to save the old growth forests in Temagami, and I wrote a song for a demonstration at the Ontario Parliament Buildings. That song was "O Mother Earth": I asked myself what I really wanted to say, and I realized it was simply "thank you." When one of the chiefs from Temagami hugged me after I'd sung it, I knew it had worked.

Honey Novick is a singer/songwriter/voice teacher/poet who facilitated the McCrae House Canada Day Poetry Event for 5

[53] "Nam Myoho Renge Kyo" is loosely translated as "I dedicate my life to the mystic law of cause and effect, resulting in universal harmony through sound." [Novick's note]

years in Guelph. She also teaches Voice Yoga. She is one of the 2020 Community Hero Awardees for creating music and poetry events and volunteering to give away free food. Since 2020, she has twice garnered the Outstanding Neighbour Award, and her Member of Provincial Parliament has nominated her for Poet Laureate of Ontario.

Mariam Pirbhai

1. How would you describe your ***relationship to the land****, and how long have you called a particular physical place 'home'?*

I was born in Pakistan, and Canada has been my home for thirty years. I've lived in Ontario most recently, so this province has been my newest discovery of Canada's landscapes. I spent my childhood in England, and some of my teenage years in the Philippines, which has given me a transcontinental relationship to the land. On my bad days, I think of the land in a schizophrenic sense, and on my good days I see it with a comparative lens. This sensibility has made me consider the way migration also occurs in the natural world, and sometimes I identify with those transplanted trees and plants!

I specialize in postcolonial studies, so I'm frequently thinking about the relationship between colonization and settlement, and the impact of this relationship on both people and land. This awareness has deeply informed my own relationship to the land, as I think of myself as another kind of settler—not as a European settler, but as an émigré-settler. For instance, I am interested in the idea of native versus non-native flora, and I've come to know that many of the plants we think are a part of the Canadian landscape are actually non-native. There's this idea of adaptation among plants as well as in cultures and people. In connection to eco-colonialism, I've become sensitive to the ways in which non-native plants have caused a kind of ecological warfare on the land.

2. Is your relationship to the land affected by any particular ***religious or spiritual grounding****, or does it come from a* ***specific worldview*** *of any kind?*

My religious background is Muslim, and that was the worldview I was raised in. Having said that, I don't feel that it has formed in me any specific sensibility or worldview about the land in particular. In fact, I would say the opposite is true—that land and nature have become my religion, or the basis of my spirituality. I find that learning about Indigenous spirituality and worldviews has taught me a lot about the intimate connection between land and people, versus other kinds of belief systems which often position human beings at the top of the ladder. Many, if not most, Indigenous cultures across the Americas tend not to see the world in hierarchical terms but, rather, see human beings as an extension of our natural environment. We have so much to learn from that. Seeing things from this perspective opens the possibility for replenishment and regeneration. We think that we can't undo the damage that we've done, but thinking in cyclical terms, and relational terms, affords the possibility of restoration.

3. What is your ***motivation and hope in writing poetry*** *related to the environment? What kind of a role do you see poetry as fulfilling?*

First and foremost, a lot of my interest in writing about place has come from my own more recent experience as a non-European émigré living outside a major urban centre like Toronto or Montreal. Whenever you come across literature by non-European émigré-settlers such as myself, it's usually set in a big metropolis. I wanted to break the mold and think about non-Europeans' relationship to rural spaces and smaller townships, instead of being constricted by the immigrant-in-the-city trope.

Another motivation comes from my growing love of place. Derek Walcott says that the poet's responsibility is to write about the land with love. He says that a traveler who writes about a place is not necessarily doing so out of love. But once the traveler stays, they're not writing in motion, but observing in *stasis*. This becomes an act of love; Walcott calls this the *eros* of home.

In many ways, I think that what I'm doing is a working love letter to Canada, and to this place within it. The more I write about it, the more rooted I feel. I'm writing myself into the narrative, and that makes me feel connected.

Mariam Pirbhai was born in Pakistan and spent her childhood in England and the Philippines before her family made their way to Canada. She is the author of a book of creative nonfiction titled *Garden Inventories: Reflections on Land, Place and Belonging* (Wolsak & Wynn, 2023), a novel titled *Isolated Incident* (Mawenzi, 2022) and an award-winning short story collection titled *Outside People and Other Stories* (Inanna, 2017). She is also the author and editor of several academic works on the literatures of the global South Asian diaspora, including *Mythologies of Migration, Vocabularies of Indenture: Novels of the South Asian Diaspora in Africa, the Caribbean, and Asia-Pacific* (U Toronto Press, 2009). She is Professor of English at Wilfrid Laurier University, where she specializes in postcolonial studies and creative writing. She lives and works in Waterloo, Ontario. Website: mariampirbhai.ca

Arwen Roussell

*1. How would you describe your **relationship to the land**, and how long have you called a particular physical place 'home'?*

I'd describe my relationship to the land as symbiotic. I honour the land with my life because my body is the land—all that I have is borrowed, and will return to the Creator later. I'm not separate from the land. When I touch my feet to the earth, I feel like I'm touching my own self. Though I'm technically a nomad, I've been in Hamilton off and on all of my life. I'm grounded in the east end of Hamilton and Stoney Creek, but also with my extended family in Chippewa on the border of Niagara Falls.

*2. Is your relationship to the land affected by any particular **religious or spiritual grounding**, or does it come from a **specific worldview** of any kind?*

Good question. Ever since I was a little kid I always asked "Who is God? Who is Creator?" As a teenager I read as many sacred texts as I could. I feel a lot of connection to the Bear teachings in the First Nations worldview: the bear walks with a slow grace, and walks in the medicine paths, for the healing of body, mind and spirit. My own mix is Cree and Mi'kmaq, through my dad being Metis. My mom was raised in the folklore of the Arawak people; she's first-generation Canadian from the Caribbean, where there are many Indigenous forms of shamanic awareness. The first religion that ever found me was actually all religions that follow both God and Jesus Christ. Even though the sacred has many names to describe itself, it is one whole--all the sacred is the sacred. So, I honour the land like a Native person, I smoke weed like a rasta, I engage in prayer to Jesus Christ like a Christian—and they all respect the land.

But my relationship to the land also comes from my own ethics: if you feel the frequencies of the earth it will talk to you, and explain itself to you. If I'm there in the forest, with medicines, and I'm singing, the spirit of the forest hears you, and will sing back. I no longer separate God and the land. The Christian bible teaches that God is in every piece of wood, every piece of something. Those who view the land as something outside of themselves, and don't do any form of prayer, are the ones who do the most bad stuff to it.

3. What is your ***motivation and hope in writing poetry*** *related to the environment? What kind of a role do you see poetry as fulfilling?*

A lot of people know me as a musician, but already way back when I was seven I started writing poetry because I didn't feel I connected with a lot of my peers. My poetry is quieter than my music, and more intimate to my core personality; it relates to my more gentle, receptive self. My main thing in poetry now is Spoken Word, and I'm used to working with that paradigm. The poem "Welcome to my Home" came out of meditating and prayer. I want to share my perspective: my core intention is to let the words I was given to say by God be respected, and to create respect in others for the land—to show reverence for everything that exists.

> **Arwen Roussell** writes, "I have been an artist my whole life, experimenting with visual, dance, lingual, and musical arts. I am grateful for this land, the medicines I have gathered from it, and the opportunity I have to feel safe here. I am Metis and have lived in the greater Hamilton area all of my life. Metis culture is based upon the mixing of French settlers and Indigenous existence, making up an inclusive, rich culture with beautiful music, food, and art to share with the world. I have always been passionate about self-healing and self-expression. I am always grateful to share my thoughts and feelings with newness and friendliness."

Bernadette Rule

1. How would you describe your ***relationship to the land****, and how long have you called a particular physical place 'home'?*

I lived in our family home in Western Kentucky till I turned eighteen. After high school, I never lived there again, though I visited often; but childhood years are like dog-years, longer and deeper than any others, so that place will always be home to me: you're imprinted with wherever you're born. I've lived in the Hamilton area now for almost fifty years, and feel bound to both my homes, Kentucky and Ontario. I moved to my present house in Dundas twenty-one years ago, and that's a record—the longest I've lived in any one home. I love this place. I feel my relationship to the land passionately—hike and birdwatch, recycle, pick up litter. Unfortunately I'm a lousy gardener. There are many trees on my plot of land, which I try to keep tidy and leave alone—which does seem to encourage a lot of birds and butterflies. Other people would turn it into a showplace, but I never mow in spring, to encourage a blue sea of forget-me-nots, and I love watching what comes in sequence after that, year after year. Those cycles are compelling for me, especially as a writer.

2. Is your relationship to the land affected by any particular ***religious or spiritual grounding****, or does it come from a* ***specific worldview*** *of any kind?*

I was raised Catholic, and I would *like* to say that my religion was the source of my love of the creation, and in some way it was: the creation to me is really the key to the mystery of spirituality, of why we're here. But sadly I cannot say that the church gave me any encouragement toward an ecological viewpoint; we didn't learn much from being kicked out of the Garden of Eden! When I was in parochial school I got in trouble for arguing against the teaching that animals don't have souls: that was always a burr under my saddle. Hierarchy is embedded in concrete in Christianity: that we are God's chosen, God's most special creature, and are above the other creatures. Yes, we're supposed to take care of them, but they're not on a level with us. I hated that. As a kid I was fascinated by whatever was growing or jumping or running past me; I've always wanted to see the sunset and the moonrise, to go out among fireflies, to see what's happening in the sky. Most people thought that was strange.

Of course that lack of a sense of ecology is not true of all religions. It's not true of Native American religions, nor of the Jains in India, who are marvellously aware of the value of every living creature. So there are spiritual teachings that do begin where we ought to, with valuing all life forms. And I *do* think the church is doing better than it was, as all institutions are, in terms of taking ecology more seriously—which we must!

3. What is your ***motivation and hope in writing poetry*** *related to the environment? What kind of a role do you see poetry as fulfilling?*

I think poetry is an extremely important art-form. All art-forms are about expressing emotion and thoughts about being alive on the planet. Poetry is lucky: it can be very brief, very concise; it's portable, sensual, concentrated, musical, and image-based—a good poem has the five senses at work in it. Joseph Brodsky says poems are stop-signs that keep us from rushing through our lives. Poetry is a kind of life-giving meditation: you stop, and you think about where you are. Wallace Stevens says poetry is a pheasant disappearing in the brush; that speaks to the peripheral, oblique nature of poetry, the way it engages the reader and makes him/her anticipate and rebuild the thought.

We turn to poetry to connect to deep emotion and to our deeper intellect. Think of how poetry is shared at gatherings like funerals where we're trying to get at some bigger issue that we need to work through together—and what's more important than ecological reality right now? Often people will remember a poem, or look it up again. A good poem has the power to make us do things we might not have done otherwise.

We've got to do something to have our collective will be realized in terms of the environment, and if poetry can help, well—besides reducing my own carbon footprint, it's all I've got to offer!

Bernadette Rule lives in Dundas, where she hikes & birdwatches, & then writes poems. She has ten collections of poems published, most recently *The Window Washer of Chartres* (Paradise North Press, 2023). She has just released her second nonfiction novel, *The Arithmetic of Color* (lulu.com, 2024). Rule received the 2017 City of Hamilton Arts Award for Writing. Her first nonfiction novel, *Dark Fire*, was shortlisted for both a Hamilton Literary Award and for an IPPY Award. *Art Waves*, her Mohawk Radio artists' interview program, is podcast at www.archive.org/details/artwaves

Doug Sikkema

1. How would you describe your ***relationship to the land****, and how long have you called a particular physical place 'home'?*

When I think about home, I think of the Niagara area because that's where I grew up, and it has always been to me the source of stability. In my mind and my imagination, even though I have a family of my own, I still think of Niagara as the home place where my storylines and family lines all connect, partially around farming. My mom's dad started a nursery in Holland and that family business has continued to today. Farming, gardening, relating to the land is bred in us through generations. My wife and I now live in Binbrook on an acre and a half, and it's becoming the place we want our kids to think of as home and become attached to. But I feel there's a tension in terms of how I relate to land or think about home places, because there should be this Christian acceptance that we're pilgrims and nothing here is permanent. Home is something where if you hold onto it too tight it becomes an idol. But I also want to push back against the rootless modernity that says that the ideal is to be home everywhere, which means you're home nowhere.

2. Is your relationship to the land affected by any particular ***religious or spiritual grounding****, or does it come from a* ***specific worldview*** *of any kind?*

Yes and yes, but it's complicated. My last few years have been spent trying to understand how Christians should view the natural world. Christianity does privilege the human person as the steward of creation, but the Bible shows that we actually aren't the centre of the universe—the story we're told is more geo- and theocentric, and humans exist between those two poles. And there's something properly awe-inspiring and humbling about that—we don't have to save the earth, God is upholding and sustaining it. What's more, creation is happening all the time: God is still speaking it into being. And it means this moment right now is a gift that we can receive, and then we have to respond. And this influences my approach to place—place is not just random or arbitrary, it's what John Calvin called the "theatre of God's glory."

I sometimes romanticize my own family's use of the land in the horticulture industry and farming. But when I look at what they *do* from an environmental perspective, it's actually quite damaging to the earth—it's very heavy with insecticides, pesticides, and chemicals. To me it's not enough for my family to have the idea of "we're all Christians and we love the land." Your worldview is your action, your religion is your behaviour. I can't just have the right idea about the environment but then participate in some of these destructive behaviours.

3. What is your ***motivation and hope in writing poetry*** *related to the environment? What kind of a role do you see poetry as fulfilling?*

In my poetry I am trying to tie my story with my place's story, which is a human and also a non-human story that precedes me—this land has always first been in relationship to God, and its value and dignity are because God is upholding it. What I love about poetry is that it's a meaning-charged response to your place. It's a way to belong to your place or make sense of how you belong to it.

A lot of the poems I think about regarding home are rooted in memory—Wendell Berry plays a lot with the idea of membership and re-membership or re-membering, and that when we memorize what came before us (even our former selves), that's another way to belong to a place. We remember who came before us, even if that person was our younger, maybe more naïve or more wicked self, and we need to learn how to hear their voices and reckon with them. We live in a world where evil is deflected onto a system, but I think a healthy understanding of evil is that it is right here inside of me. I don't hold the hope that literature or beauty is going to save the world—but I do think it can *address* evil, and maybe part of restoration can happen that way.

Doug Sikkema grew up in Southern Ontario amidst vineyards and peach orchards, limestone ravines and great lakes. He earned a B.A. in English from Redeemer University, an M.A. in English Literature from the University of Ottawa, a B.Ed. from the University of Toronto, and a Ph.D. from the University of Waterloo. His current work explores the relationship of religion, literature, and the environment in contemporary literature. Doug is an assistant Professor of Core Studies and English at Redeemer University, an editor of *Front Porch Republic*, Board Chair of Oak Hill Academy, and Senior Research Fellow with Cardus … and an aspiring gentleman farmer in Binbrook, ON with his wife and four children and two canines.

Jennifer Tan

1. How would you describe your ***relationship to the land****, and how long have you called a particular physical place 'home'?*

I have lived in Hamilton for more than 30 years. I am aware that though Hamilton has problems with transport and traffic, greenery surrounds us and the area is known for waterfalls. As for myself, I would say that ever since I was a child I have been fascinated by plants, their beauty and the many ways they propagate themselves. In school, I was chosen to be the president of the Science and Nature Society for two years, even though I had avoided dissecting frogs and worms.

Over the years I have lived and worked with people of many different races and nationalities. I have a South-East Asian background: my parents were both Straits-born Chinese, which means we don't speak Chinese but instead a mix of Malay and Hokkien, resulting in something like patois. I am interested in other languages too, especially in Spanish and French. Hamilton's demographic has been changing as newcomers move into the city: we can appreciate a growing and vibrant mix of diversity here, with all its varied cultural attributes. It is like a garden with a variety of plants in bloom.

2. Is your relationship to the land affected by any particular ***religious or spiritual grounding****, or does it come from a* ***specific worldview*** *of any kind?*

I heard about Rachel Carson's *Silent Spring* about 50 years ago from my schoolteacher when I was in secondary school in Singapore, and have been conscious of the environment from a young age. We are fortunate to have clean drinking water when there are others who do not. We have to be responsible stewards of the land we live on, because the future of our planet will be devastating if no one cares.

*3. What is your **motivation and hope in writing poetry** related to the environment? What kind of a role do you see poetry as fulfilling?*

People have been writing about flora and fauna for a long time, but these days poets are offering more eco-poetry. People generally want to be entertained rather than preached at: though they are easily moved when they listen to music or are captivated by images of flowers or puppies, mere words and reasoning will fall on deaf ears. With my poems, I hope that my readers will get a sense of wonder and go on to imagine beyond the words when they reach the last line. If the truth in words has a sound arrangement that carries a rhythm, it comes alive, and hopefully the reader will catch on to it too. When writing poems relating to the environment, I find myself appreciating nature that lets me breathe, eat and drink from it. Through writing I get further insights and a certain rhythm to my thoughts. I find that when a poem is finished it can be quite satisfying. I can be surprised by words that want to get out and come alive.

Jennifer Tan was a committee member for Hamilton's LitLive Reading Series and was the coordinator for LitChat, the literary salon, for many years. She is a regular supporter of and contributor to the Tower Poetry Society. Jennifer won the Short Works Prize for poetry in 2016 and in 2020. She has many indoor plants.

John Terpstra

1. How would you describe your ***relationship to the land****, and how long have you called a particular physical place 'home'?*

I have lived in Hamilton for about fifty years, although I wasn't born here. During all that time, and through several moves, without knowing it, I have stayed within the watershed of Chedoke Creek. Then suddenly I am doing research and writing a book about the creek. It makes me wonder if it's true that the land, the earth, has agency, and I am inclined to believe that it does—even, and perhaps especially, in the city.

When a natural geography becomes married to a built geography, the built generally dominates the relationship. The natural goes into hiding. Your relationship to it must become more conscious and intentional, and investigative. It's not handed to you on a plate, as it seems to be when you're camping or canoeing on a lake. But the secret benefit is the pleasure of knowing that you and the land are in it together.

2. Is your relationship to the land affected by any particular ***religious or spiritual grounding****, or does it come from a* ***specific worldview*** *of any kind?*

The further I push forward, the less willing I am to see a separation between myself and nature and the built environment. Part of my religious grounding was in the Creation story of Genesis, a story that I imagine as being told around a campfire by people trying to give shape to their experience. The story is definitely on the side of things being "made." As a maker (in wood), I am also on that side.

"All we are is story," writes Thomas King. The opening line of the Gospel of John reads, "In the beginning was the Word." I wonder now if the world we see around us, the rock, trees, water, etc., are each forms of speech, different languages, that we must learn to hear and understand if we are to enter and tell the story.

The genius behind the Garden of Eden story is that it places the responsibility for the way things are, all the imperfections and challenges, on human beings: it doesn't let us off the hook. My personal theory is that we should spend half our time making a living, and playing, and the other half of our time cleaning up after ourselves.

Christianity has often been lax and criminally negligent in not trying to integrate itself into any new landscape, or to understand the spiritual realities of the people who are already there. In Ontario, the Haudenosaunee Great Law of Peace and their Thanksgiving litany, at the very least, have a world to offer, that is literally grounded here.

3. What is your ***motivation and hope in writing poetry*** *related to the environment? What kind of a role do you see poetry as fulfilling?*

I don't consider that I'm writing *about* nature when I'm writing something that *includes* nature. The separation between me and the world around me seems to be thinner than it was before, so I'm just writing about the world I'm living in, rather than writing consciously about "the environment." But I do bear witness to places, and features of the landscape (as we call them) and historical events, which have voices that are out of range for most of us, and so we cannot hear. I am one of those writers whose subject chooses them, rather than the other way around, so when I write about Chedoke Creek or the Iroquois Bar (both in Hamilton), it's because they have tapped me on the shoulder and suggested I follow. Is that even possible? To be approached like this? It is a question, again, as to whether or not the earth speaks, and has agency. The answer to which lies partly in whether one sees the earth as living, or inert. Poetry can give voice to what we've lost, what we mourn, as a result of what humanity and industrialization have done to the landscape. Poetry is also privileged to still have access to the Garden, and to speak of this transcendent, down-home beauty and largesse, which persists in spite of it all.

John Terpstra's poetry and prose often circles around the landscape at the western tip of the easternmost Great Lake. Over the course of fifteen published works, he has covered the ground, walked the streets and followed creeks, and has been short-listed for and won awards in both poetry and creative nonfiction, from the Governor General's to the Charles Taylor to Hamilton Literary Arts. One of his poems in this collection, "Giants," is inscribed on a plaque on the edge of the Niagara Escarpment overlooking downtown Hamilton.

Elizabeth Tessier

1. How would you describe your ***relationship to the land****, and how long have you called a particular physical place 'home'?*

I've lived my entire life in Hamilton—I'm a born and bred Hamiltonian. We used to spend summers up near Port Dover at a cottage and that's where I felt the most connected to land, but my mother has a long heritage and history in this area. Her relatives were the first white settlers on the Grand River. That part of her settler history was horrifying and embarrassing to her because she had deep concern for Indigenous issues and injustices that were committed, and recognized her family involvement in that. The sole ancestor she found some affinity with, Jerusha Currie, seems to have developed relationships with her Indigenous neighbours who helped her carry on running the family farm after her husband, oldest son, and last child all died within a year. Those family members that died are buried in the brambles on the side of the Indigenous cemetery. All of Jerusha's kids went to the local school on the reserve, and it's rumoured one of her daughters was in class with Pauline Johnson.

My ancestors' relationship to the land was less connected than the Indigenous peoples', and mine is much less connected than my mother's was. She grew up on a farm with no running water, could tell by looking at a roast what part of a cow it was, and planted anything and it grew, whereas I barely stay within civic ordinances with my garden. I'm not a gardener, I'm writing poems. There is an element of removal from nature that I experience.

2. Is your relationship to the land affected by any particular ***religious or spiritual grounding****, or does it come from a* ***specific worldview*** *of any kind?*

I'm always interested in our relationship to land and to God, what that means, how it changes. I think there's something about human nature that's fairly constant, but our experience of the world can change over time a lot, so what can we learn by looking at the lives of others? I have an M.A. in religious studies from McMaster University; I lost my religion doing my M.A., but I never lost my spirituality, and one of the texts I studied, *The Cloud of Unknowing*, was very inspirational to me. The contemplative author says that we can't have knowledge of God in our reason—it's only through love that we can experience God, and even then there's always a cloud between us and God, but striving for that cloud is the work of the contemplative. So I guess that's how I see myself.

3. What is your ***motivation and hope in writing poetry*** *related to the environment? What kind of a role do you see poetry as fulfilling?*

Reflecting about what we learn from the past, things we value, things we don't value, what gets saved, what gets discarded is very much a part of my poetry. To me the important part of the poem is to open up an experience for the reader in a new way. The early English-Canadian author and naturalist Catherine Parr Traill initially wrote about how to struggle against the wilderness, but near the end of her life she became an environmental activist, questioning what settlers were doing to the world around them, such as cutting down irreplaceable trees. It's pretty telling that the settlers themselves saw that we were creating a monster. What things can we see about our own relationship to the land and our ancestors' relationship to the land that we want to keep and that we want to change? What will our descendants write about us in 100 years—about our relationship to the land?

Elizabeth Tessier is a Hamilton poet. Her work is informed by her 30 years working in Hamilton museums and her current life with early onset Parkinson's. She has previously published in *Evenings on Paisley Avenue: Seven Hamilton Poets*. She has a self-published book, *The Words They Cannot Say*, edited by her friend and mentor Marilyn Gear Pilling. Her chapbook *Frozen Charlotte* is published by Frog Hollow Press, edited by Shane Neilson as part of their Dis/Ability series. She has had work in RAVE and the Spring 2021 *Hamilton Arts & Letters*, thanks to her friend, inspiration and editor Bernadette Rule.

Anna Yin

1. How would you describe your ***relationship to the land****, and how long have you called a particular physical place 'home'?*

I have always had a close relationship to the land. In Chinese traditional poetry, the landscape is always there, and it also reflects the poet's mood. In the vast land of China, the style is different from north to south, like the landscape. In the north the land is very open and high, and the poetry seems grand and high too. In the south there are small mountains and lots of little villages, so the poetry is more tender, softer, and more private. My poetry feels like that kind of poetry which is intimate. But Canada is now home to me because it is so beautiful, the air is so clean, people are friendly and open. I have lived in Ontario for 20 years. I have enjoyed writing poems about Canada, especially when I was Mississauga's Inaugural Poet Laureate—my job was to write poems about our city and to promote the literary arts.

I want to travel around Canada and visit the lighthouses for their histories and their symbolic meaning in Canadian landscape. To me they are "life jars," like many other quiet places you can find even in a city. Inside the life jars I imagine fireflies, like the ones I used to catch in the Chinese countryside as a child. I also like walking on the trails around the shores of Lake Ontario; there are often signs about nature and creatures in that area, reminding us to respect and care for our environment. Every day when I take a walk on the trail behind my house, I am happy to listen to many birds singing beautifully. I was amazed to find out such wonderful bird names, so I wanted to write a poem about them.

2. Is your relationship to the land affected by any particular ***religious or spiritual grounding****, or does it come from a* ***specific worldview*** *of any kind?*

I have no specific religion, but I do believe in harmony and balance in nature, as Yin and Yang are balanced in Chinese thinking. Chinese traditional medicine believes that to make illness go away you need to adjust and find harmony. I have personally experienced significant physical healing through relaxing, eating healthily, and taking daily walks on the trail. When I go to nature every day, I always feel refreshed. I'm not materialistic: I don't need much money to be happy, and I believe that if people can avoid that kind of peer pressure, they can find more harmony and be more peaceful. For a couple of years, I would read or write a haiku every day before work to relax; haiku have become a kind of meditation for me. These kinds of practices originated from Chinese traditional poetry and Chan Buddhism, which influenced Japan as Zen; it has the whole idea of letting go and being humble in nature—as you quiet yourself, you can truly see other things. I am also open to learn and respect other worldviews. I was touched by one line from the Bible that tells people to look at the birds, because birds do not worry: nature is just so generous, to care for all of us.

3. What is your ***motivation and hope in writing poetry*** *related to the environment? What kind of a role do you see poetry as fulfilling?*

Working as an I.T. professional, I use my spare time to read and write poetry. In fact, poetry saved me after I had two miscarriages: it brought me hope when I was depressed. Now I have published six books of poetry. In my writing, landscape is always there too. When I write poems, the images usually come to me first—I guess that made it easier for me to write haiku later. After I started writing haiku, I turned more closely to nature. Haiku are a way of living mindfully by slowing down and fully paying attention. I wanted to share my experience, so I started leading haiku workshops which invite others to slow down and experience the richness of being in each moment in nature and writing about it, and the healing that comes from that. Poetry in general has the role of healing and strengthening the human mind and bringing peace and joy, which is why I design and lead Poetry Alive workshops for the public.

From Chinese culture-rooted landscape to the new and welcoming Canadian landscape, **Anna Yin** has found her home in poetry and authored five poetry collections and one collection of translations. She won the 2005 Ted Plantos Memorial Award, two MARTYs, two scholarships from the USA and three grants from the Ontario Arts Council. Anna was selected as Mississauga's Inaugural Poet Laureate. Her poems/translations have appeared in *Queen's Quarterly, ARC Poetry, The New York Times, China Daily,* and on CBC Radio. She has performed on Parliament Hill, at the Austin International Poetry Festival, and at the Edmonton Poetry Festival. She continues exploring landscapes through Poetry Alive workshops with multimedia. She can be found at annapoetry.com and contacted at anna.yin@gmail.com.

CODA

Tranquility[1]

1 Sharon Trottier is a registered psychotherapist and art therapist who has worked with local and Northern Indigenous clientèle. Sharon is extremely proud of her Bay of Quinte Mohawk ancestry, which she can trace back to the 1700s. She lives in Hamilton. 'Tranquility' is acrylic on canvas, 12" x 12".

THREE HAMILTONIAN CITY POEMS

Steel City in Winter

Each step I take sinks nearly through the concrete
Skin of the city: wheezing, exhaling steam
From factories no longer familiar with it.
The railroad cuts along the spine of the city;
Something living seeps out on either side.

One day everything will crumble into the bay—
    A synthesis, a turn towards fluidity.

On the edges of all of this, the trees hang over us like lace
    The light cuts through the grey like stained glass
    And a finch perches on daisy stems, once dead.
On the edges of all of this, a deep green breath waits for me,
    Standing at the intersection of the ancient and the industrial
Two thoughts playing across my mind.

Magda Teeuwsen
Editorial assistant

Witness

You stand, all ash and empty
heart, your scars a violence to my eyes.
I grow upon your feet, a persistent, useless
presence, like a dying man denying death—
          I'm a witness to your wounds.

There's smashed glass against
your wood, fires lit within
your roots   the faces I'll never find
burned out all the weight within your trunk. And I cry,
for your gravity to be gained, for your strength to
grow green within the burns, to crush the hands
that gouged your heart.

Yet benign, you do not sway, your
silence holds a love I cannot learn—
        in strength, you gather height,
        and grow into the light.
And in the spring, I'll come to hear your
voice, leaning in the wind, your words
a whisper on the leaves. Your scars
the ridges for my spine, firmer than
the ground from which we've grown.

Renessa Visser
Editorial assistant

Acknowledgement at the Corner

We are gathered on a street corner,
in a city where land meets water,
under a wall of rock;

where brick from the clay of its soil,
and quarried rock,
have become the walls of our homes,

on streets that run through fields and orchards
planted on the traditional territory
of the Haudenosaunee and Mississauga nations,
Anishnaabe and Wendat-Huron,
on lands protected under
the Dish-With-One-Spoon wampum agreement—

whatever our blood or background, our belief,
whichever street we live on,
we share this dish …

John Terpstra

AND A LAST WORD

Sacred Trust

We are the keepers of this land

She shelters and sustains us

Long after the flesh fails the spirit

We will care for these lands

Our drums will be heard upon the winds

Our voices in the rustle of the leaves

My people have a sacred trust with the land

A trust no man may break, a trust that
death cannot sever

We were here when you first stepped foot
upon this land

And here we will remain long after the last
step has disturbed her soil.

***

"The poem 'Sacred Trust' was written from the perspective of my people but I believe it should be a vision of all people and a statement that should be made when you become a new citizen of this country."

—**Chief Stacey Laforme**, *Living in the Tall Grass: Poems of Reconciliation*

Acknowledgements

This project has been several years in the making. I'd like to acknowledge fine research and editorial assistance from Elise Arsenault, Liane Miedema Brown, Magda Teeuwsen, and Renessa Visser, and in particular all kinds of editorial involvement, over and above, from Noah Van Brenk.

On the journey, we've received helpful input, support and suggestions on various aspects of the draft manuscript from Margaret Bienert, Rick Monture, Paul O'Hara, John Weaver, the folks at Publication Studio Guelph, and a number of the poets, with special thanks to Gary Barwin. Deep gratitude also to Brian McHattie for his generously-shared wisdom about Indigenous history.

We are grateful for illustrations from a raft of fine photographers: particularly Lynn Bergsma Friesen, who has produced the bulk of the photos, but also John Bowen, Linda Frank, Liane Miedema Brown, and Shannon Nelson. Many thanks to Tamara Watson for the clear and attractive map of our area, and to Mohawk artist Sharon Trottier for her permission to reproduce her picture "Tranquility."

I should also recognize generous financial support for four years from SSHRC, the Social Sciences and Humanities Research Council of Canada.* This funding has been vitally necessary: without it, there would be no anthology. Many thanks too for both administrative and collegial support from staff and faculty at Redeemer University.

I have been ongoingly grateful to Michael Mirolla at Guernica Editions for guiding us through the whole publication process, as well as to Errol F. Richardson for lovely and creative work on the visuals and formatting. These folks have been a treat to work with.

And of course most of all I want to say a heartfelt thankyou for ongoing support, astute insights, and regular cheering on the sidelines from John, without whom nothing.

Deborah Bowen
August 2024

* *Poetry in Place* is supported in part by funding from the Social Sciences and Humanities Research Council.

Social Sciences and Humanities Research Council of Canada
Conseil de recherches en sciences humaines du Canada

Canada

Illustrations

1. Cover photo: Victoria Park, Kitchener.[1] Credit Lynn Bergsma Friesen[2]
2. Map of 'Land Between the Waters.' Credit Tamara Watson[3]
3. Squirrel closeup. Credit Lynn Bergsma Friesen
4. Landscape off Hwy 6. Credit John Bowen
5. Hamilton Harbour in winter. Credit John Bowen
6. Cedar tree-roots. Credit Lynn Bergsma Friesen
7. Red-tailed hawk. Credit Lynn Bergsma Friesen
8. White-tailed deer. Credit Shannon Nelson[4]
9. Male Blue Dasher dragonfly. Credit Lynn Bergsma Friesen
10. Queen Anne's Lace. Credit Linda Frank
11. Mennonite farming. Credit Lynn Bergsma Friesen
12. Mixed-colour beets. Credit Liane Miedema Brown
13. 'Lake-baby.' Credit John Bowen
14. Monarch butterfly. Credit Lynn Bergsma Friesen
15. 'Tranquility': painting of deer. Credit Sharon Trottier[5]

Poets' headshots.

Several poets requested that we credit their photographers:

Adam Dickinson:	credit Scott Turnbull
Joanne Epp:	credit Anthony Mark Schellenberg
Catherine Graham:	credit Marion Voysey
David Haskins:	credit Chris Pannell
John Terpstra:	credit Jeff Tessier

---

1 The name 'Victoria Park,' encumbered as it is with the history of colonialism, has brought calls from Indigenous land defenders to reclaim the natural culture of the park by renaming it Willow River Park. This issue is unresolved at time of publication.

2 Our chief photographer, **Lynn Bergsma Friesen**, writes that she spends as much time as possible outside exploring the beauty all around us with a camera in hand. She also has the privilege of being a teacher in Kitchener, Ontario.1 The name 'Victoria Park,' encumbered as it is with the history of colonialism, has brought calls from Indigenous land defenders to reclaim the natural culture of the park by renaming it Willow River Park. This issue is unresolved at time of publication.

3 **Tamara Watson** is a Hamiltonian graphic designer and mother of three.

4 **Shannon Nelson** lives on a farm in mid-western Ontario with her husband and dogs, and really enjoys photographing the sights around her beautiful area.

5 **Sharon Trottier** is a registered psychotherapist and art therapist who has worked with local and Northern Indigenous clientèle. Sharon is extremely proud of her Bay of Quinte Mohawk ancestry, which she can trace back to the 1700s. She lives in Hamilton. 'Tranquility' is acrylic on canvas, 12" x 12".

Copyright permissions and acknowledgements

Madhur Anand. “We’re Not Worried,” “Somewhere, a Lake,” “Will it?,” “Bell Curve,” and “Evan Said” from *A New Index for Predicting Catastrophes* by Madhur Anand, copyright © 2015 Madhur Anand. Reprinted by permission of McClelland & Stewart, a division of Penguin Random House Canada Limited. All rights reserved. Any third party use of this material, outside of this publication, is prohibited. Interested parties must apply directly to Penguin Random House Canada Limited for permission.

Mia Anderson. “All We Know of Angels” reprinted from *Practising Death* (The St. Thomas Poetry Series, 1997) and “O Emmanuel” reprinted from *O Is For Christmas* (The St. Thomas Poetry Series, 2024), both by permission of the publisher. “Dear Arne & Marie-Françoise” reprinted from *Appetite* (Brick Books, 1988) by permission of the publisher. “Hibiscus” reprinted from the opening poem of a long poem sequence from *The Shambles* in *The Malahat Review* 100 (Fall 1992) by permission of the author; “Rhubarb” reprinted from *The New Quarterly* 159 (August 2021) by permission of the author.

Fitsum Areguy. “beyond the fridge” reprinted from the art installation “Gaukel Block ‘on unseen hands / / stories of care’,” with art by Conan Stark (Kitchener, summer 2023), by permission of the author. https://conanstark.com/gaukel-block-kitchener

Gary Barwin. “Escarpment (Autumn)” and “Invisible Deer” reprinted from *For It Is a Pleasure and a Surprise to Breathe: New and Selected Poems* (Buckrider Books/Wolsak & Wynn, 2019); “Commencement for Cootes Paradise” reprinted from *The Dalhousie Review* 100.3 (Autumn 2020); all by permission of the author.

Anna Bowen. “How to Love a Landfill” reprinted from *Re:Mediate* (PS Guelph, 2016) by permission of the author.

Daniel Coleman. Epigraph to Section 5, "Wild Creatures," reprinted from *Yardwork: A Biography of an Urban Place* (James Street North Books, 2017) by permission of the author.

Linzey Corridon. "A French-Canadian, but not really, moves to Hamilton" reprinted from *Hamilton Arts and Letters* 14.1 (2021) by permission of the author.

Corri Daniels. "Forest Songs" reprinted from the *Chapter House Journal* (winter 2022) by permission of the author.

Adam Dickinson. "The One Virtuous Act of the Dictator," "Disappointment in the Masonry," and "Beetroot" reprinted from *Cartography and Walking* (Brick Books, 2002); "Father Demetrius's Bees" and "The Egg as Immigrant" reprinted from *Kingdom, Phylum* (Brick Books, 2006); all by permission of the publishers. "Hail" from *The Polymers* copyright © 2013 by Adam Dickinson. Reproduced with permission from House of Anansi Press Inc., Toronto, www.houseofanansi.com

Joanne Epp. "Hilton Falls" reprinted from *The New Quarterly* 122 (Spring 2012) by permission of the author.

Jaidyn Fenton. "Amherst Island," displayed as part of an installation at the Art Gallery of Hamilton, 2020, reprinted by permission of the author.

Linda Frank. "A Philosophy of Zoos," "Divided," "Sweet," "Dragonfly," and "Orb Weaver" reprinted from *Divided* (James Street North Books, 2018) by permission of the publisher.

Marilyn Gear Pilling. "Home" and "Heaven" reprinted from *A Bee Garden* (Cormorant Books, 2013), and "Eye of the Farm," "Looking Out," and "In the space of ten minutes" reprinted from *The Gods of East Wawanosh* (Cormorant Books, 2019), all by permission of the publisher.

Catherine Graham. "Breakwater" and "American Woodcock" reprinted from *The Celery Forest* (Wolsak & Wynn/Buckrider Books, 2017) and "Escarpment" reprinted from *Winterkill* (Insomniac P, 2010), all by permission of the author.

David Haskins. "Reclamation" reprinted from *Tamaracks: Canadian Poetry for the 21st Century* (Lummox, 2018); "For My Friend Who Grows Peaches" reprinted from *This House is Condemned* (Wolsak & Wynn, 2013); and "Pruning Black Raspberries" reprinted from *Blood Rises* (Guernica Editions, 2020); all by permission of the author.

Cornelia Hoogland. "Li, The Clinging, Fire," "Ko, Revolution," and "Chung Fu, Inner Truth" reprinted from *Cosmic Bowling* (Guernica Editions, 2020), all by permission of the author.

Karen Houle. "Woodland Occupation of North Dumfries Township," "Apoid Wasps," "Roma," "Mennonite Wife Prayer: Chokecherry," and "Controlled Burn: Phragamites" reprinted from *The Grand River Watershed: A Folk Ecology* (Gaspereau P, 2019), all by permission of the publisher.

Greg Kennedy. "Psalm 46" reprinted from *Reupholstered Psalms: Ancient Songs Sung* New (Novalis, 2020) by permission of the publisher; "Swifts," "September: Hay Fever, Hogwash, and Goldenrod," "The Barn," and "Healing our Harrowing" reprinted from the *Ignatius Farm Newsletter* by permission of the author.

Paula Kienapple-Summers. "Sunrise Over the Grand River" reprinted from *Fresh Voices* #22 (League of Canadian Poets, April 2021) by permission of the author.

Gimaa (Chief) R. Stacey Laforme. "Sacred Trust," "Mother Earth," and "The Day the Earth Cried" reprinted from *Living in the Tall Grass: Poems of Reconciliation* (UpRoute/Durvile Publications, 2017) by permission of the author. "Climate Change?" reprinted from *Love Life Loss and a little bit of hope: Poems from the Soul* (UpRoute/Durvile Publications, 2024) by permission of the author.

Janice-Jo Lee. "Ancestor Song," SOCAN 2023, reprinted from YouTube at https://www.youtube.com/watch?v=pqJy-WCI7OU and "Still of the Lake," SOCAN 2020, reprinted from BandCamp at https://folkadelphia.bandcamp.com/track/still-of-the-lake, both by permission of the author.

John B. Lee. "Talk of Trees," "The Lost Hawk," "What Suffers into Shadow at the Edges," and "Elegy for Al Purdy" reprinted from *This is How We See the World* (Hidden Brook P, 2017) by permission of the author.

Tanis MacDonald. "A Feminist Guide to Reservoirs" reprinted from *Sweet Water: Poems for the Watersheds*, ed. Yvonne Blumer (Caitlin Press, 2020); "How to Get Lost in Your Backyard" and "Syrinx" reprinted from *Straggle: Adventures in Walking While Female* (Wolsak & Wynn, 2022); all by permission of the author.

Kate Marshall Flaherty. "Goose, Plummeting" and "Triptych for One Loon" reprinted from *Reaching V* (Guernica, 2016); "God's Bits of Wood" reprinted from *Titch* (Piquant P, 2003); all by permission of the author.

Geoff Martin. "Somehow, Potatoes" reprinted from the final issue of *The Olive Press* (Issue 7, 2019) by permission of the author.

Daniel David Moses. "Crow Out Early," "Dandelions at Dusk," and "The Corn" reprinted from *The White Line* (Fifth House, 1991) by permission of the author. "Some Grand River Blues" reprinted from *Sixteen Jesuses* (Exile, 2000), and "Buzz" and "The Orchard Song" reprinted from *A Small Essay on the Largeness of Light and Other Poems* (Exile, 2012), all by permission of the publisher.

Honey Novick. "Mushquoteh" reprinted from *Ruminations of a Fractured Diamond* (Lyricalmyrical P, 2011); "Oh, Mother Earth" reprinted from *New Songs for Peace* (Creative Vocalization Studio, 2000); both by permission of the author.

Paul O'Hara. Epigraph to Section 3, "Trees," reprinted from *A Trail Called Home: Tree Stories from the Golden Horseshoe* (Dundurn P, 2019) by permission of the publisher.

Mariam Pirbhai. A version of "Not Your Garden Variety Stories of the Grand River Watershed" appeared as "Not Your Garden-Variety Settlement Story" in *Garden Inventories: Reflections on Land, Place and Belonging* (Wolsak & Wynn, 2023), reprinted by permission of the author.

Bernadette Rule. "City with a View," "October Cornfield," "Food Chains (for Cathie)," and "Looking for a Fast Buck" reprinted from *Full Light Falling* (Image, 1998), and "Sequoyah" reprinted from *Gardening at the Mouth of Hell* (West Meadow P, 1996), all by permission of the author. "The Meaning of Starlings" reprinted from *The Weight of Flames* (St Thomas Poetry Series, 1998) by permission of the publisher.

Ragan Sutterfield. Epigraph to Section #8, "Farming and Gardening," reprinted from *Wendell Berry and the Given Life* (Franciscan Media, 2017) by permission of the publisher.

John Terpstra. "Giants" and "To God, as a Small Pest" reprinted from *Two or Three Guitars* (Gaspereau P, 2006); "The Highway That Became a Footpath" reprinted from *Brilliant Falls* (Gaspereau P, 2013); and "Invasive Species" reprinted from *Call Me Home* (Gaspereau P, 2021); all by permission of the publisher. "The Kind of World We Live In" reprinted from *Wild Hope* (St Thomas Poetry Series, 2020) by permission of the publisher. "Place" reprinted from *Naked Trees* (Wolsak & Wynn, 2012) and "Acknowledgement at the Corner" reprinted from *Hamilton Arts and Letters* 13.1 (2020), both by permission of the author.

Robin Wall Kimmerer. Excerpt from "The Sacred and the Superfund" from *Braiding Sweetgrass: Indigenous Wisdom, Scientific Knowledge and the Teachings of Plants*. Copyright © 2013, 2015 by Robin Wall Kimmerer. Reprinted with the permission of The Permissions Company, LLC on behalf of Milkweed Editions, milkweed.org.

Tamara Watson. Designer of map of Land Between the Waters, with map data from OpenStreetMap (openstreetmap.org/copyright).

Printed by Imprimerie Gauvin
Gatineau, Québec